WILLEM de KOONING

Willem
de KOONING

by Thomas B. Hess

Distributed by Pocket Books, Inc.

GEORGE BRAZILLER, INC.

NEW YORK   1959

LIBRARY OF CONGRESS CATALOG CARD NUMBER: 59-12224

PRINTED IN THE UNITED STATES OF AMERICA
BY R. R. DONNELLEY & SONS COMPANY

CONTENTS

De Kooning in his studio, around 1938. The *Seated Man* in the background was later painted out

Willem and Elaine de Kooning, June, 1950

De Kooning's studio, 1951, *Woman I* in background

De Kooning and Franz Kline, Springs, L.I., 1956

The will to a system is a lack of integrity.
                                          NIETZSCHE

IF, FROM a bird's-eye view, you could watch the artist walking through
the years of time across the country of his art, Willem de Kooning's
journey could be compared to one that Kafka described in a letter to
Klopstock:

If we were on the right road, having to leave it would mean endless despair. But
we are on a road that only leads to a second one, and then to a third one, and so
forth, and the real highway will not be sighted for a long time—perhaps never—
and we drift in doubt, but also in an inconceivably beautiful diversity; so the ac-
complishment of hopes remains an always unexpected miracle, but in compensa-
tion, the miracle remains forever possible.

But this view would be inaccurate as it ignores what one critic calls de
Kooning's Michelangelesque "ambition," which is an even more inade-
quate phrasing, because "ambition" has connotations of power that are
irrelevant to de Kooning's attitudes. Had the critic said "Michelangelesque conscience," he would have had a point: conscience as a devouring
necessity to create "impossible" new "masterpieces"; conscience as a
hand with a knife that destroys an endless number of paintings when,
in the moment of doubt, despite the "inconceivably beautiful diversity"
of their forms, they do not incarnate the habitually unexpected, but
incessantly demanded miracle—an art that can be anything and everything.
    De Kooning's paintings are based on contradictions kept contra-
dictory in order to reveal the clarity of ambiguities, the concrete reality
of unanswered questions, the unity of simultaneity and multiplicity. He
does not aim at complexity nor mystery nor exploitation by indirec-
tions; he aims straight at the mark—to grab the real by the throat. But
reality itself—the reality of art and the place of this reality and the role
of the Artist and his life as just another guy who faces art and other
artists and looks from a man's-eye view at the country across which artists

7

walk—is impossibly complicated and ambiguous. And to reach it, an artist like de Kooning, who is fully aware of being an artist, must use the "impossible" weapon of reality itself, the specific truth. And truth can be touched only by complications, ambiguities and paradox, so, like the hero who looked for Medusa in the mirroring shield, he must study her flat, reflected image every inch of the way. And if this image was a political cartoon, the label in Perseus' hatband might read:

The Crisis of Modern Art

CRISIS ALWAYS has been the one faithful companion to the serious artist in America; and, since around 1925, it also has been dogging serious artists in Europe. Crisis may change costume every now and then, but its pressures remain constant. It is an accessory built-in to the American scene.

De Kooning's career has developed in an environment—New York City since 1926—marked by four changes in as many decades. To oversimplify, there was the esthetics of the 1920's, the Depression years and Social-Realism, the "release" from politics and the efflorescence of abstract painting in New York in the 1940's, and its consolidation (and colonization) in the 1950's.

In the 1920's the problem facing the artist was distorted by the naïvete of the American art world. The crisis in modern art that was driving Paris delightfully mad had only vague echoes in New York, where the interior push was apt to be simply: "How to Get Out of Town?"

De Kooning, arriving from Holland in 1926 (biographical details are in the Chronology), had no contact with the personages of the twenties—Marin, Weber, Hartley, Demuth, Pach, Davies, Lachaise, etc. He was meeting artists whose directions, like his own, were not yet settled.

But behind its innocent reflections in the American scene, the crisis of modern art was manifest in Paris, where succeeding waves of painters' inventions were less and less available to young artists. For example, at the crest of the moment of 1925 was Surrealism; in painting it was represented most distinctively by such artists as Magritte, Tanguy, Delvaux and Dali, who never were able to execute successful large pictures. The Surrealists who did work "big," Picasso and Miró, were peripheral to the intellectual core of the movement as defined by its most creative doctrinaires, the poets Breton and Eluard. But note, this was the first time in Paris that the Great Painter was not at the center of "his" own movement.

Instead of centering movements, the Paris masters continued to

8

work in the seemingly endless springtime of their culture; living in grow-ing isolation from each other, they began to "close-off" their images. Before, there had been ample room for young artists to work in between the idea of the master's painting and its finished appearance. Painting is an intellectual action (viz., *all* great painters have been good writers) that can express a whole philosophy. The image of the paintings them-selves may not completely expose the philosophical premises, just as the writings of Kierkegaard or Coleridge never exhausted their insights. This openness attracts other artists, and, in time, may create schools and conventions. On the other hand, certain painters, like certain writers, can express themselves so fully that there is nothing anyone can do with their images except to blend indistinguishably into them or to explode. By the mid-1920's the masters of Paris painting were filling out the images of their art to the limits. The crisis of modern art rapidly was defined in terms of: "What Is There Left to Do?"

Word of this malaise was slow to reach New York in the 1930's. In the pages of the lush French magazines, which were America's main contact, the new was announced in the same magisterial accents with which Apollinaire had ushered the Cubists on-stage. Americans still were involved in the process of catching up, but because so many ideas about painting had been used only locally, in the way that a manufacturer might "use" an astronomer's idea to plan an assembly-line for the mass-production of headlights, almost nothing appeared to be "closed-off" for good; everything remained to be re-thought from scratch (a process that de Kooning, an expert at giving stereotypes a good kick, always has enjoyed). Mondrian, Cubism, Ingres and Courbet were not the only ones to tempt radical New York revisionists. The Renaissance, the Greeks, all art history was seen as fresh material for insights. They wrote Mal-raux's books fifteen years before he thought of them.

The social patterns of the 1930's were set, like wind sets ice in a pond, by the freezing "conditions that prevail" (to quote Durante)—economics and left-wing politics. Dialectics and historical necessities had everybody by the elbow and showed him to a new bench where he could "work" "productively"—for somebody else. The crisis got a name—"Crisis." But it was a crucial period in American painting, one that un-fortunately has been neglected.

With the Depression came the inauguration of government-spon-sored arts projects which channeled New York painters and sculptors into social groups. Where there had been culture-cliques—the Stieglitz Circle, Henri's students—based on ephemeral task-ideologies, by the mid-1930's government subsidies had created an "artificial" beehive state for artists; its structure was not particularly weakened by the fact of its economic artificiality (i.e., money did not come through the art-market; in fact from the 1930's to the early 1950's, none of the New York artists ever expected to sell pictures as European artists do—with enough profit to live on). A true *esprit de corps* emerged, a sense of seniorities, colleagues, and of an Audience. The Audience was composed largely of other artists, but it was big enough to respond and it worked so well that, ever since, American painters have created their own publics. For it should be noted at this bleak Depression point, that the American mass public always has been violently hostile and contemptuous of modern art.

In America the crisis of modern art in the 1930's was still a dim mirroring of the actual situation that was centered in Paris, where the bankruptcy of Surrealism as a program and the completion of the "closing-off" of the great masters' images was evident to anyone who knew how to look. The masters themselves paused, as though to catch a breath before their final spurts of tremendous energy. Their followers (and who were the bright new lights in 1935?—Fautrier, Lam, Fougeron?) were painfully discovering that the crisis meant: "There Is No Place Left to Go."

However it seemed as if there were too many places to be in at the same time in New York. The jabber of radical politics filled the vacuum. "Everybody," everybody said, "has his role," history was casting daily. The Painter should enlighten the People; the dialectic of burnt umber should be conditions of servitude, and alizerin crimson agitates for Tom Mooney.

Naturally few good artists were trapped by this rhetoric, although its constant reiteration must have created a generally manic neurasthenia. Still, it is one thing to laugh when a painter dashes into a meeting, fresh from the Midwest—dustbowl courier—and shouts, "Nobody cares about van Gogh!" But if he really is saying, "What can you do with van Gogh or with Picasso or with Miró or with anything?"—then he has a point. The shovings and exhortations of American painters by radical politicians may have been absurd, but *by coincidence* they touched the real and usually unmentioned dilemma of the artist.

The results of this coincidence were stupendous. Miles of federal wall-space were decorated with abominable "wage-slaves," a billion pop-eyed, square-toed (Aztec-Rivera protocols) figures with surly, triangular little faces whined for bread and soup. And much excellent work also was done, unfortunately most of it was lost during the reaction against the whole period which came in the 1940's. The liquidation of ideologies brought a huge sigh of relief from the artists. At last they were free to paint—in fact to be artists, and to enter the crisis of modern art first-hand or single-handedly. Paris, which once seemed so distant, had

10

either been sealed off by the Nazi Occupation or had arrived in New York by Pan American clipper.

In 1958 a group of French critics angrily wrote that "The New American Painting" was initiated wholly by Paris painters, sculptors, poets and teachers who were in New York in the 1940's. There is a fraction of truth to the claim. Léger, Miró, Ernst, Chagall, Ozenfant, the Surrealists, all were around New York at the time and familiarity bred familiarity. The Americans learned two things: Parisians like Breton or Masson are human beings, perhaps brilliant, perhaps a bit stuffy, but with pores and hairs; and, furthermore, they acted as though Art were a distinguished, honored profession that included poetry, music, theater, little magazines and the bullying of museum directors in its purlieus. Art was a way of life that, far from being an "anti-progress," ivory-tower position, took in the whole intellectual world. And it was at this moment that a series of American painters burst into new styles, most spectacularly and publicly Jackson Pollock, who threw himself head-first into abstracting Expressionism, creating a focus for the avant-garde, making himself famous, becoming by an act of will The Greatest Artist in the World. By 1950 there were about twenty painters deeply and successfully involved in the issue. Painting, it seemed, would be a new kind of autobiography, which would be universal through its depth, but uniquely individual at the same time—each explorer to his own bathosphere.

The social structure of artists in a community of artists, as defined in the 1930's, was maintained. But, in de Kooning's words, "Jackson Pollock broke the ice." Later de Kooning qualified this by pointing out that he was using a characteristically American phrase to indicate a typically American event. Actually Pollock was of little help to other painters except, in a few cases, as a model of risky deportment.

The direct influence of Paris painters on the New York situation for the most part was very slight. Such artists as de Kooning had taken everything they could use from Picasso, the early Kandinsky, Miró, Mondrian or Soutine since the 1930's. But the colorful *Surréalistes et Cie.* emigrés certainly were an important part of the enthusiasm of the mid-1940's.

It took about six months for serious art students, and about six years for serious collectors, to be attracted to the new kinds of American painting. The students were helped by the fact that Hans Hofmann was running an influential school, and that many of the other New York painters, to support themselves, had to teach (de Kooning worked a summer semester at Black Mountain and an academic year at Yale).

The exploitation and colonization processes were in full swing by the mid-1950's. As soon as a painting was finished, museum and univer-

11

sity trainees would accept, classify and tag its look. Sainte-Beuve's dream of a Botany of Intellectuals had come true. The social protest inherent in modern painting—its essential aspects that shock or startle or disgust at first sight—was muffled in a "big yes" of specialized professional taste (that only de Kooning's Women have been able to contradict since). And if a painter like de Kooning made some pictures that were a bit too difficult to be understood immediately, his followers diluted the concept and made it readily available in a matter of weeks.

Meanwhile artists in their twenties and thirties kept appearing in the late 1940's and through the 1950's, giving a sense of active continuity and scope to the New York scene. Older artists, in their late forties and fifties, continue to surprise (if sometimes only for an instant) by their ability to face and overcome the changing crisis of modern art.

The Dark-Horse Tic

WITHIN THIS background (highly schematized here), de Kooning, like his colleagues, moved along his own twisting paths and shortcuts. In the 1920's he was finding a style and a place in the milieu. In the 1930's his European brand of radical anarchism and political sophistication made him an antagonistic part of the generally Communist-oriented activities of American intellectual circles. Like his friend Gorky, he faced painting, and the crisis of painting directly—although de Kooning's works of the Depression years, grayed rose, melancholy figures, men in dusty work-clothes, sometimes scarred, mute, prematurely aged, capture the texture of the period; indeed they are, I believe, its most poignant embodiment.

American painting, since the time of Benjamin West, has been the Dark Horse of the European art world. Europeans always had demanded, and Americans, being Europeans, tried to fulfill the idea of an American culture—whether *Pantisocracy* for Coleridge or *Amerika* for Kafka. The Romantic notion of the American Dark Horse finally "making its move" at the turn to "win" a race became, by repetition, an American chauvinistic habit—almost a cultural tic—which de Kooning has called "Eating John Brown's Body" (i.e., coming from nowhere to become, by proclamation, The Champion). But it always was obvious to artists like de Kooning and Gorky that such "moves" were futile and that modern art is international and cosmopolitan. And as de Kooning did not participate in the "typically American" movements of the 1930's and early 1940's, he was considered an odd-ball by the artistic community. He had the reputation of not reading the proper Marxist excerpts, not caring enough about The Social Issue of the Month, and not finishing paintings with expected regularity. But he had his own circle of friends in the 1930's—writers, poets, musicians, painters, some

12

of them regularly bought his works for what was a livelihood then, but seems very little now—no one had much money at the time.

In the 1940's there was another Dark Horse move in American art, this time with Pollock, Baziotes, Rothko, Still, Gottlieb, Hofmann, etc. A foreign observer visiting New York in 1944 easily might have considered it just another manifestation of the familiar cultural tic: there were enthusiastic and eloquent critics (notably Clement Greenberg and Robert Motherwell), hyperbole, strong attacks from the official spokesmen of the Establishment, apparently an organization of sorts, programs, jeers at Paris, officialdom and, in some instances, at the artists' own immediate past. De Kooning was not a participant in these activities; he refused an exhibition at Peggy Guggenheim's gallery (to which William Putzel, her perceptive advisor, had invited him) on the grounds that he was not "ready" (by the artist's own standards, he is never "ready" for an exhibition) and he shied away from most of the uptown celebrations and infighting.

Downtown, where the artists lived and worked and visited each other's studios—which was, and is, the only real "organization" that has ever existed—he became a hidden *chef-d'école*. His abstractions seemed to *be* what many other artists were driving at, or seemed to indicate ways out of impasses. And because he was apart from the public arena, and because Bohemia prizes its secrets as much as any other section of our tribal society, de Kooning became a numinous leader among the New York avant-garde artists—without even trying. Of course he has the basic charismatic requirements. De Kooning is an engaging conversationalist with highly original viewpoints; he is interested in what other people are doing; he speaks his mind freely, listens intently; he has an aristocrat's sense of irony and manners; he enjoys social events. These attributes helped de Kooning become, willy-nilly, "the artist's artist" of 1942-48, and they probably acted against him just as sharply in the 1950's when he found himself with so large a number of followers that only a Mohammed could have welcomed them.

De Kooning's reputation in the public art world (i.e., among informed museum officials and dealers) was established almost immediately after his first one-man exhibition in 1948. By the end of the 1940's and in the early 1950's, he took part in a number of the many panels and symposia the artists were organizing with increasing frequency—a kind of semi-public auto-criticism. He was still an odd-ball insofar as any system for artists was concerned, fanatically anti-fanatic, against all group-efforts, propaganda, programs. But his odd-ball position, partly due to his own eloquence and leadership, partly because it was becoming evident that this stance was one of the few tenable ones left for an artist, became a kind of programless program. Plenty of people came along five years later with the time and pedantry to spell out exactly

13

how programless a programless program should be, although, as is to be expected, each plank in their platform was strictly anti-de Kooning.

The Dark Horse move of American art in the early 1940's was not another desperate plunge from the far turn, but the real thing, and despite attempts to institutionalize it, to give it ready-made names, slogans and enemies, it soon presented itself as an international and cosmopolitan phenomenon, with all the energy and self-awareness such a moment implies. Influenced and influencing, de Kooning was a part of the moment. He was in an atmosphere where what he was doing was taken seriously. He could receive and give ideas. There was an expansive sense of life, even if living itself for a long time remained marginal.

It would be misleading to imply that New York was a skyscraper "happy hunting ground" for artists in 1945–55. Certainly no society has been tougher on its intellectuals, especially on those whose success is not spelled out in headlines. And consistent with this soft-headed Philistine approach, most American museums and collectors seem to find a perverse, if subconscious, pleasure in encouraging the imitative while ignoring the creative. But it would be equally false to suggest that each new American artist to emerge during the decade 1945–55 was a lonely hunter—like Ryder, Allston or Vanderlyn, Americans driven mad in the blank jail of total public incomprehension.

The Moving Target

DE KOONING'S CONSCIENCE, as has been suggested, is Michelangelesque. He has not tried to fit his art in between other artists' ideas and their pictures, but has insisted on making the painting that would completely express his ideas and engage his entire methodology. Logically, this is a shaky situation, because ideas and methods develop in reference and in range during the execution of each painting, which is one reason, perhaps, why so many of de Kooning's works are, according to the artist, "unfinished" or unrealized. De Kooning's is a slippery universe made of expanding numbers of indications and changing points of view—a finished painting is turned upside-down at the last moment, an eye becomes a tack, a thumb becomes a mountain. Man, traditionally the measure of all things and whom all things measure, goes around systematically breaking every platinum yardstick he can get his hands on.

Nothing seems constant until the artist's œuvre is viewed as a whole, at which point it becomes evident that de Kooning's is a cumulative, mnemonic art that is all of a piece—a continually growing edifice of memory and invention.

The crisis itself enters the content of the painting; forms and meanings exfoliate; multiplicity becomes a premise. The clarity is that of ambiguity. Realism is a metaphysical position—something like Courbet's *Realisme,* or Giotto's—a means to break through accepted Style to find, as if for the first time, an order in things as they are—the human figure, the human scene, as it is. "Nothing is less clear than geometry," de Kooning once wrote. Life as we live it, obviously, is a matter of endless ambiguities and proliferating meanings; transparencies upon transparencies make an image that, while it blurs in superimpositions, takes on the actuality of rocks.

The dialectic between the revelation of this mystery and the ordering powers at the artist's command is, I believe, the content of de Kooning's art.

It is important to keep in mind that de Kooning's art is all of a piece. It is necessary prosaically to dissect its various elements for discussion. But in their life as facts, the paintings never appear as sums of elements; their unity is their breath.

Throughout his career de Kooning has invented, enlarged and perfected an extraordinary repertory of shapes, some simple, some complex, and in the work of inventing and perfecting them he has gone back continuously to older shapes, re-creating new ones from them, as if he were impelled to bring a whole life's work into each section of each new picture. One is reminded of *delectatio morosa,* the temptation to which medieval monks were susceptible, an obsession that comes from a profound and sustained concentration on recurring forms and ideas—the idea becomes a part of the thinker's body; he returns to it over and over again. And one is reminded of Ingres, like de Kooning an encyclopedic draftsman, who, once he had established the turn of the bather's neck or the set of her spine, would rephrase the shape with constantly re-inspired variation for the rest of his life.

Perhaps when, like Ingres or de Kooning, an artist is able to invent his own form, the shapes themselves retain the energy that went into their creation and they store it like coal stores fire.

Harold Rosenberg recalls a conversation with de Kooning in the 1930's in which the artist spoke of Cézanne's admiration for Mallarmé, and described how Cézanne had taken over the poet's use of the multiple meanings of words to paint a tablecloth that also would be a mountain. And certainly de Kooning developed his repertory of shapes in a similar way; each invented shape changes in a new context but it never sloughs off any of its old significations. Suggestions become more and more dense, more and more textured by the variety of concepts and contexts within them. But de Kooning could not "use" Mallarmé's idea, as Cézanne had been able to. The crisis of modern art presupposes that each shape, even a plain oval, be re-invented—or, rather, given an autochthonous existence in paint. Nothing could be accepted or received

15

on faith as a welcomed heritage. Everything had to be discovered and then assimilated—from the *table rase*.

A number of the artist's works, particularly from the years 1930–40, can be "read" as little "dictionaries" of motifs. Almost every shape in the later abstractions is stated in a realist context in portraits, figure-pieces, still-lifes, in thousands of working drawings and in two commercial jobs he executed, one for the New York World's Fair in 1937 (plate 15), the other for the Container Corporation in 1944–45 (plate 70). But two points should be underlined in any use of paintings as vocabularies to interpret other paintings: first, the shapes cannot be read "backwards"; second, signs cannot be re-interpreted as symbols. In the Container Corporation picture, there are elements in the façades of Dutch buildings, in shutters and doors, in weathervanes and steeples, in the clock, windmill and the windmill's counter-weight, in the pole festooned with streamers, in the way space is pushed vertically up and down the streets and houses, that may be recognized in abstract works of a later period. A shutter appears in *Light in August* (plate 68), a heart in *Valentine* and *Little Attic* (plates 74, 107), a weathervane in *Black Friday* (plate 95). But although it is probable that the shutter-shape itself derives from recollections of Holland, as do the windmills and Gothic weathervanes, the re-invented shapes are also parts of anatomies or of spaces in the structure of picture-building. The paintings are never riddles to be solved by correctly following a chain of clues or by naming the "real" root of a shape. Secondly, a common motif in the early paintings is the egg. In our myth-ridden age of do-it-yourself archetypal analysis, Egg might be interpreted as Mother, thence to Clytemnestra, born from an egg, to Orestes, etc. Such an "explanation" makes as much sense as referring Egg to the impression made upon the young artist by big American breakfasts.

Once they are defined, de Kooning's shapes stand for themselves, retaining all their meanings and contradictions, but they are never letters in an alphabet from which words can be spelled.

A Few Motifs

THE EGG: it appears in the earliest pictures as a still-life object whose ovals can fill a painting, as a village of huts, or a head. When it loses its identity as Egg, the oval remains insistently in faces, eyes, breasts, a light-bulb on a table, a pure shape that might be a lamp globe or the top of a glass seen from an angle or an apple. At some point in this process the oval enters de Kooning's mind and eye as a possession that, just because of its ability to multiply meanings, can be used anywhere he wants to put it. He has liberated the shape from the crisis (in which

16

the problem would be stated in such terms as "ovals are finished, they all belong to Arp and Miró") by inventing it. It is an autonomous piece of his world. When the oval appears in later paintings, it is a "de Kooning oval"—fruit, face, flower—it can be anything. (Plates 6–15, 17, 19, 35, 38, 47, 56, 60, 68, 78, 90, 96.)

The vertical stripe: this also enters de Kooning's œuvre very early. It is the edge of a wall or the base of a table, a mast for an egg-boat, a stake, a tree trunk, a chimney stack, a banded vertical related to the maypole-like stanchion in the Container Corporation advertisement or to a barber-pole. (Plates 6, 7, 10, 12, 15, 48, 50, 55, 58.)

Drapery: the folds, pleats and creases in old clothes or in a curtain tacked to a wall behind a figure have been a rich source of invented shapes. Notice how some dents and lumps in a pair of work-faded and stiffened pants will take on the heart-shape from a Dutch façade, or how a tablecloth becomes a mountain after all, and the worn clothes themselves turn into the skin over a new kind of anatomy, until a whole painting loses itself in this fascination. The tacks and nails that hold the draped curtains to a wall—little spurts with heads—become cousins to buttons and buttonholes, laces, eyes. (Plates 17, 18, 22, 25, 32, 37, 38, 40, 41, 60.)

Other motifs: the whole repertory probably can be "named" by examining the early works and their subsequent assimilation in the œuvre. Space prevents a detailed account in these pages, but the reader might be interested to follow some preliminary indications for himself:

A table top: plates 6, 10, 12, 18, 20, 44.

A vase: plates 9, 10, 11, 13, 19, 22, 32.

A chair: plates 9, 10, 22, 25; the arm of a chair: 33; a sofa: 58, 59, 66.

Matches bent out of a matchbook: plates 56, 100, 102.

There are innumerable others which I hope to consider in a longer book on the artist. Five major themes, however, because of their importance, may serve to introduce as many aspects of de Kooning's concepts, and may clarify the dialectical role that ambiguity plays in his paintings: a window, drawings, "intimate proportions," letters, spaces between shapes.

Inside-Outside

THE WINDOW appears in de Kooning's work at the beginning (plates 9, 10); a face peers out of the window (plate 12); a window is drawn to an upper corner by the mutual attraction of right-angles (plate 11); it is suggested in the rectangle made by overlapping transparencies (plate 17). The window's frame picks up the beat of the painting's quadrangle. The face looking out of a window becomes a painting on the wall (plates 34, 35), or a window becomes a mirror (plate 37), or a window with the shades half-drawn is also a painting on a wall and a piece of glass on a shelf (plates 50–53). The rectangle is cornered inside the painting to become the stabilizing anchor for the curving shapes (plates 54, 55). It is also the division between the space of indoors and outdoors (plates 57, 59). It is the window of a house seen from the outside and, simultaneously, the window inside a room (plate 60). It mirrors other shapes (plate 67); reversing them, it reveals them. You see the landscape through a window (plate 88), but if it is really a mirror, the scene is reflected from behind you, and you are in a landscape. In some "interiors," particularly the *Boudoirs* (plates 103–105), a figure sits in front of a mirror-window-picture. In the stages of *Woman I,* photographed during its metamorphosis (plates 111, 112, 114, 115–117), the changes made in the "window" emphasize the ambiguity—or, better, the growing scope—of the scene. Place swells to include all places. It is a concept which de Kooning once nicknamed "no-environment." The window-outdoors-indoors-mirror-painting-rectangle is its embodiment.

The Question of Where

No-environment—the metaphysical and social alienation of man from society and the nightmares of urbanization have been a preoccupation of modern writers from Marx and Dostoievski to Heidegger and Céline. For de Kooning, however, "no-environment" is a metaphysical concept with physical materiality—with flesh and cement. In the Renaissance, he has pointed out, the painter located a Christ and a Roman soldier in their appropriate "places." What is "place" today? A glance at a newspaper photograph or television report shows an incident in a city street that also might be happening in an open field, or Hollywood Bowl. The *details* by which our environment is measured and given philosophical scale are no longer reliable optical indices to the question of "Where?" The window near *Woman I* indicates that she is sitting indoors, but she could equally well be on a porch, or outdoors near a wall. The porch and the wharf, places in between, are the starting points for "no-environment," they are inside and outside, land and ocean.

Inhabiting "no-environment" are the quasi-anonymous objects it has bred: a dress on a hangar or on a clothesline, a decanter on the lawn or a table, an angled wall turning left or right above the horizon. And details from the artist's own "no-environment," his studio, are translated into the picture space: a label, a sign, a window seen from a window, a box on a shelf. The poet Frank O'Hara once met de Kooning on the street, the painter said that he had been out "buying some environment" for a picture; under his arm he had a box of drugstore cotton.

"No-environment" is not a generalized, idealized, sociologically observed phenomenon for the artist. It is where he lives (where we all live); it is the place of his studio and its environs, where he paints, and stops to look out of the window, sits down, takes a walk . . .

The studio and its appurtenances have entered painting with increasing strength of presence since Chardin; with the Cubist collage, the studio itself began to invade the serious picture. Things taken off a wall or picked up from a work-table became the subject of the image, or the image. One of the decisions many New York artists made in the 1940's was to have their painting mean anything and everything. From this it followed that the studio should be everywhere and anywhere. The painting and the studio, the streets outside, the drive through the country that led away from and back to the easel, all merged into the painting—especially de Kooning's, who played a leading role in this decision.

Drawings on the Floor

A STREAK of blue in a de Kooning painting might come from the blue of a box of cotton or from the label on a carton of breakfast food in a corner of his studio, or from a piece of oil cloth lying in the backyard which his studio windows overlook. But it also could come from a drawing and de Kooning's studio is filled with and haunted by them. I can think of no painter since Ingres whose intellectual powers have been brought to bear so insistently and methodically on the act of drawing. And drawings enters the painting as a basic part of the "no-environment" in the complicated oval of the artist's field of vision.

A piece of paper is one of the first motifs in de Kooning's painting. It may be an old newspaper (or a drawing?) left on the street (or on the studio floor?); it is crumpled (plate 17). Later the drawing in the picture may be a drawing for part of the picture itself, tacked to the wall or pinned next to the easel (plates 62, 73, 93). Some collages are made entirely of drawings and sketches that have been cut up and re-assembled. Other works are paintings *of* sliced and torn paintings and drawings, pinned and tacked and taped together (plate 97), and of the landscapes and figures and environment that the drawings analyse.

De Kooning draws continuously. As Valéry wrote, it is a way of thinking. The line meditates, criticizes, corrects; it becomes masses, absences, colors. Four drawings for *Glazier* (plates 28–31) are details of the process: the head changes position, a shoulder inches out, concentration gnaws at a section of drapery. His one drawing of a nude from a model (plate 44), of 1936, became a matter of infinitely corrected, invisible, hard-pencil lines. The portrait drawings (plates 24, 25, 27) have a similar obsessional attraction—the shadow that a lens throws on the fleshy

19

part of the nose rendered with a needle of graphite. "It's the kind of drawing you can lose your mind in," the artist once remarked, "I gave it up."

De Kooning draws with ink, charcoal, pencils, brushes, palette knives, spatulas, pastels, crayons, oils on rag-paper, board, old pieces of wrapping paper and endless pads. In the relentless search for form, drawings are cut apart and stuck together in different combinations, one face on another neck, legs on a different trunk. This creates a jump in space where the drawings meet, and de Kooning says that his wife first pointed out that this jump was carried over into the paintings themselves—like the "impossible" transition between the upper lip and the mouth in *Woman III* (plate 122). Sliced drawings also are placed in the painting itself. He is apt to shift a whole picture an inch inside the canvas, and, to "test" corrections, he may make a drawing on wrapping paper of a part that is to be moved (plate 118) and place it directly in the painting (see stages of *Woman I*). *Two Women* (plate 110) is a palimpsest of these "skirmishes." The ways in which the painting is observed and corrected becomes a look of the painting itself.

Drawings remain in the image as shapes painted where drawings had been taped to the canvas, and in edges and transitions, long after they have been discarded. Once they have left the picture they remain in the studio, becoming part of the "no-environment," scattering around the ship-shape floor like crazy lilypads on a hardwood pond. Later they will be neatly stacked away in portfolios, as well-thumbed as favorite books. And as such they may re-enter the paintings again, tacked to the wall behind *Woman;* torn and cut apart again they suggest new departures, but the departures keep the hereditary intonation of the parent drawings.

Drawings of drawings on tracing paper laid on top of each other at different angles pull apart the anatomy of *Woman* into a landscape, and the changes are fixed in individual studies (plates 132–134). Nothing is left to chance, although hazard is persistently introduced by the artist in order to judge all the possible permutations of his form. The painting is anything and everything, it is a piece of the "no-environment" itself, a part of nature, devouring art, chewing up drawings which enter into the bone and muscles of its structure.

Concerning Proportion

THE DRAWING is "of" something—a fold of denim, a waist, another drawing—usually it is "of" the human figure. The classic theme of a man or a woman as a hero or heroine in the tragedy or comedy of art is the touchstone of de Kooning œuvre. Like Siamese twins, his abstract pictures live off the figures; the figures cannibalize the abstractions.

20

Hands in the figure-pieces of the 1930's blend almost imperceptibly into abstractions (plates 36, 55); a thumb and thumbnail re-appear in vectors of color (plates 140, 141). *Mailbox* and *Attic* (plates 75, 106) remember thighs, breasts, armpits, mouths and eyes (eyes which are also tacks holding drawings to a wall); a smock over a belly becomes an illegible "shape."

The concept of clarity in deliberate ambiguity is brought to bear on the idea of the human anatomy—it is a sort of "no-environment" of the body which the artist has called "intimate proportions." Just as there is no real "place" in the modern environment, in the sense that a place can no longer be identified from its parts, so there is no "real" anatomy in terms of the style and proportion of details. Sections are multiple, interchangeable, in a way like American gadgets. The second joint of the index finger, seen close, could be a thigh, or a neck; the shin could be a forearm, elbows could replace knees. Style has been drained off; what is left is a cluster of related shapes, all of them vitally important in terms of their actual functions, and all of them needing rediscovery in the cool light of the artist's scrutiny. "I need to have everything there," de Kooning has said; if there is to be a woman, she must be complete. Style cannot blur the fact of the human presence, or of its own integrity outside art.

The artist has indicated, only half jokingly, that his Women are sisters to the giant ladies (girls?) that are pasted on mailtrucks and billboards—enormous public goddesses of droll sex and earnest sales-pitches. He also has pointed out that the Women are masked by the "American smile"—that ubiquitous, vacant, friendly, distant, polite expression (in one sketch for *Woman,* her smile was cut out of a "T-zone" ad for Camels in *Life* magazine). There is grandeur in this high-comedy quality, in the off-beat Dionysiac grin. De Kooning's *Women* are queens; tipsy, trullish, hiccuping with Byzantine dignity, rulers of a country that names its hurricanes "Hattie" or "Connie."

De Kooning's sense of ambiguity—or poetic insight, to give this vision a more accurate name—attacks anatomy at its most conventional, most style-filled point, at the conventional notion of Proportion. The artist re-creates each new relationship for himself at the cleared-off table where his drawings are made. An ear, the nape of the neck are thought through by the moving pencil or brush as phenomena experienced by all the senses except the eye's. De Kooning starts by drawing a knee as a knee might draw itself, then as if it were seen for the first time, and then (here ambiguity re-enters) as seen by an eye sophisticated to the whole history of art. The knee or the nape are salvaged from the crisis of art by a knowledge of styles so thorough that it can impel a new, logical configuration to appear out of the willed chaos of possibilities.

In the late 1930's de Kooning used to complain ironically that hair

21

was impossible to paint (plate 49) and that the shoulder was a ridiculously planned part of the body. Elbows were passable, but shoulders . . . the inefficient way they work, the idiotic way they look . . . Edwin Denby wrote a poem partly based on de Kooning's argument:

THE SHOULDER*

The shoulder of a man is shaped like a baby pig.
It terrifies and it bores the observer, the shoulder.
The Greeks, who had slaves, were able to hitch back and rig
The shoulder, so the eye is flattered and feels bolder.

But that's not the case in New York, where a roomer
Stands around day and night stupefied with his clothes on
The shoulder, hung from his neck (half orchid, half tumor)
Hangs publicly with a metabolism of its own.

After it has been observed a million times or more
A man hunches it against a pole, a jamb, a bench,
Parasite he takes no responsibility for.
He becomes used to it, like to the exhaust stench.

It takes the corrupt, ectoplasmic shape of a prayer
Or money, that connects with a government somewhere.

The shoulder is discovered (plates 22, 28–31, 39–41), defined, exists to enter the thrusting angles of the later paintings as a component with enough identity to be independent. It is a process of validation.

"Intimate proportions" exist in a "no-environment"; the new anatomy is a part of the new place: a special sign under which the paintings travel. And just as a thumb, knuckle and nail curved behind a ring-finger turn into a façade of still-life objects in a landscape of shelving and a flight of angels (plates 22, 24, 35, 36, 52, 55, 60, 62, 73), so the regal *Woman* turns into panorama (plates 138–140). Their faces had always opened to fields and mountains (plates 130, 134, 136). "Intimate proportions" spread to let the wind of a hill as you drive under it come through to fill the image; and a shoulder or a smile become the sense of place where a Long Island horizon or a Tenth Street cafeteria had been felt to live.

Letters without Words

DETAILS OF place and anatomy must be made neutral enough to enter the painting, but still retain their specific identity and dignity as things with the aura of life. Of all things common to the "no-environment," letters are the most intimate, supple and specific. They are objects which

* Edwin Denby, *In Public, in Private,* Decker Press, 1948.

are non-objects, angels engraving the Lord's Prayer as they dance on the head of a pin: the letters of signs, ads, signatures, Tenth Avenue grafitti, a jotted note, sky-writing (BEER, 1,000 feet long, ineffably dissolving in the blue haze of the city).

De Kooning had studied lettering at the Rotterdam Academy, and his jobs in the 1930's included sign-painting (he has used the sign-painter's "liner" brush from time to time ever since). He is fascinated by the quality a letter has that signifies a shape, a sign, a precise idea or style. Even a letter without type has a complex ambiguity of meanings and meaninglessness. I think of E M C; it could be part of the phrase "see McCrae," or the beginning of the Einstein Theory formula, or a journalist's abbreviation for "master of ceremonies," or nothing, or everything.

In the late 1930's de Kooning based some abstractions on simple words lettered across the canvas and then painted out in sections (plate 52) until the detritus letters became apples and lamps, ovals and shelves, signs and compartments. By the mid-1940's letters themselves are in the paintings; they have not left it since. If you look at *Open Road* (plate 69) from all angles (and it is necessary to look at all de Kooning's pictures from all angles); it might spell E M H L O h I, or 1 4 0 7 H M 3, and so forth, through various combinations. *Zurich* (plate 72) spells A R T. *Orestes* (plate 76) spells R A P T coming out of an O and an O-or-E. *Boudoir* (plate 105) has its B. Letters are part of the landscape-still-life-drawing details strewn over the picture as clues to the "no-place" where Woman is. In *Easter Monday* (plate 145) V, A, E and L set-off the interacting forms, turning into squared windows, elbows and breasts, walls and lakes, in a shimmering multiplicity. In the 1958–59 pictures, A, Y, K and L, enlarged to human scale, appear, disappear, re-appear like tutelary divinities of the landscape place.

In a sense what happens is the reverse of Rimbaud's famous sonnet on the "alchemy" of vowels. The letter, freed from any duties, is a shape that is perfectly familiar and perfectly new. (There is a small black-and-white painting with the letters Z O T in it. De Kooning was surprised and a bit disappointed when the late Curt Valentin asked him, "Oh, have you been to Zot?" But it turned out that Valentin was referring to a well-known spa on the Belgian-Dutch border. "Could you be referring to Zoute?" asked the artist.) The unalphabetic letters are bits of life.

Spaces in between

ONE OF THE WAYS de Kooning works is like the technique sign-painters use to paint letters. They lay a rough quadrangle of color or gold leaf over the outlined letters, and then the background is painted out to the edges. The letter is what has not been touched. The "object" is the "back-

23

ground." De Kooning paints the shapes of background and foreground, actor and setting, until they blend into one concept; the painting is unified as an organism is a unity—parts do not exist. This is seen most easily in the white-and-black paintings (plates 76–80). They are equally black and white; it is impossible to tell what is "on top of" what. There is no ground against which a shape appears. There is no place where you could say, "this is in between."

De Kooning meets the crisis of modern art (that stipulates an ethical "flatness" in painting and then adds that "flat" is an academic notion), by saturating the picture with his own shapes. He recaptures complex illusions of depth by making the image all of a piece; with no pauses or rests, no in-betweens. The artist finishes a picture as the image becomes complete, as it assumes its own "countenance"; all separate shapes are obliterated in the form. As he has said, "I paint myself out of the picture." When the artist is finished, the picture begins its own life.

In defining this concept of space, de Kooning also discovered another source for his repertory of motifs. Distance "in-between" becomes a "thing" in itself: the distance between the arm and the chest in *Classic Male* (plate 39) or the cusps between kissing ovals (plates 48, 53) are given the same energy and are as painstakingly reinvented as the shapes of shoulders. The shapes discovered "in-between" are used in other pictures, taking on the changing character of the artist's changing form. A clue to *Merritt Parkway* (plate 5) is found in a drawing of the space between an arm and the torso of a *Woman,* just as the black shapes (or the white ones) "in-between" white ones (or black ones) in *Attic* or *Dark Pond* are clues to *Woman I.*

Backgrounds and foregrounds still exist, but they are consistently interchangeable. There is a Gordian fugue of ambiguities.

The Color of Matter

DE KOONING'S COLORS share the consistent quality of his œuvre. He settled on his favorites (or they chose him) early in his career; they have been modified with changing forms and surfaces, but they have always kept a family likeness.

A pink appears in the early 1930's, and has remained one of the three key hues ever since. It is an off-beat color, between the chalky tones of the earth pigments, and the mineral brightness of the chemicals. De Kooning's pink tends more towards red than brick dust, more towards clay than neon. On certain damp nights, the sky over Times Square is steeped in it. Grayed, it tends to violet; when yellow is added, it becomes a searing orange. In some early works it has the quality of a

Pompeian fresco; in some late ones it has a startling "flesh" look—a waxwork color, face-putty. From the beginning there also has been a range of yellow ochers which lightens to bright cadmium yellow and darkens to burnt umbers and siennas—wet rust reds. Its value is often keyed to the value of the pink's; they are so close in tone that in a black-and-white reproduction they seem identical. Completing the triad is a cerulean blue, tending to green as it grays, and to a cool candy blue, very pure, very far from violet, at its most intense. Like the pinks, the ochers and blues seem to fall in between the chemical and earth pigments, they are from a no-man's land, neither animal, vegetable nor mineral. The blue in its middle cerulean register also is apt to be toned to the intensity of the pink for violent contrasts that (in Fairfield Porter's words) make your eyes rock.

Of course, de Kooning has never restricted his palette to this triad. A flat, acerb green appears in some *Women* of the late 1930's and in the 1959 pictures. In the colored abstractions of the mid-1940's, deep reds, lilacs and felt-greens are crushed like jewels in the machinery of the black-and-white action. But in general colors are based on those of land, flesh and sky: earth running easily to sun yellow, flesh to blood-red, sky to ocean-blue or the equally mysterious blues of overalls and the wall-paper in rooms of half-destroyed buildings. This has been consistent from the subdued, almost timid, early statements to the grand wide ges-tures that follow.

Color never sticks out oddly on top of the composition, as it some-times does in Picasso or Miró, nor drenches form as in a Bonnard. It is there in an absolute way, without "style." De Kooning likes to think of his colors as being based on "the most banal and obvious" sources. But just as the *Women* are "cousins" of the billboard goddesses and yet pro-foundly more regal, the colors, too, glimpsed in the common common-place environment, in the usual vulgarity and melodrama, achieve a new ambience of vibration and light. The light of New York, and the light of ethics.

Edwin Denby wrote in a sonnet subtitled "The designs on the side-walk Bill pointed out":

> The sidewalk cracks, gumspots, the water, the bits of refuse,
> They reach out and bloom under arclight, neonlight.

Flesh and sky slap down on top of each other with the thrash of a hailstorm. Earth and water come so close that the tossed-in sun simply joins the drama. Colors erupt through the ceiling, coherent in their poetry of ambiguity. Here de Kooning's metaphor approaches Rimbaud's famous sonnet.

The surface, the flesh of the painting itself, reflects and expresses the concept of ambiguity in crisis. De Kooning can make a big painting in a day, scrape it off in a few minutes, paint it again the next day—a painting a day for a year on the same canvas. He never paints over old pictures to get the rich, slightly simple-minded look that Picasso has made so popular. De Kooning always keeps the surface fresh, painting up from clean canvas or paper. But if you paint on the same canvas over and over again, ghosts of old pictures begin to haunt it, the anguish of destruction remains evident even when the strokes are debonaire enough to make a fencer tip his hat.

In early pictures the paint is smooth, even and thin. Sometimes de Kooning sand-papered it or rubbed it with rags. Often it looks polished. When a heavy impasto appears (plate 47) it has the presence of a bas-relief, like a collage, and a sense of calloused flesh. The pigment comes off the brush smoothly to the surface; control is a premise. As control is perfected, the range of textures increases. Pigments become thicker, they flow faster. Islands and dunes appear and disappear. There is erosion and eruption. Around 1945 the artist used some inexpensive house-painter's enamels in black-and-white pictures (where colors appear, they are regular tube pigments). The speed of surface effects increases (the painter John Ferren once estimated that de Kooning's "whiplash line" travels at 94¼ miles per hour). Once de Kooning was able to sell a few paintings, the colors became thicker and more expensive (the equation may seem shabby, but such is the formula in the "culture center of the world").

There is a haptic ambiguity where drawings or overlays, or remembrances of drawings and overlays, make visual jumps and "impossible" confluences. There is freshness, clarity and control, and there is a sense of horror, a brutality about the paint itself—an aristocratic lack of squeamishness, and also a sense of tragedy and hopelessness. Paint will clot in lumps of dead or dying matter—a garbage-choked river. The moment of despair in the studio, in the "no-environment" that gulps a whole culture, is fixed in the scarred, over-used paints. A smell of death hangs over the bounce and feel of life, over the cheerful offset-images of guys and dolls from the movie-sections of newspapers that were put on a painting to keep it from drying too fast—a sense of reality beyond Art, the pulse of life, destruction and duration.

A Roll of Dice

"THE ONE indispensable psychological condition for any esthetic doing," Nietzsche wrote,* is a "frenzy of will—the tremendous drive to bring out

* *Götzen-Dämmerung*, translated by Walter Kaufmann (Viking).

26

the main features." But along with the "Dionysian frenzy," Nietzsche insists that there must be habits of seeing—"accustoming the eye to calmness, to patience, to letting things come up to it; postponing judgment, learning to go around and grasp each individual case from all sides."

To use ambiguity, simultaneity and multiplicity in the continuing crisis of modern art, calm and frenzy must alternate, possibly in split seconds. The issue in the moment or hours of calm is to purify and test the frenzy, a point raised, I believe, by Harold Rosenberg's epithet Action Painting as it is applied to de Kooning, Pollock and others. The painter acts in the arena of his canvas, and constantly judges the results of his action. His correction or rejection of a gesture in paint becomes an ethical decision. What is rejected was not true to the experience that formed and sustained the act. The question immediately arises as to how much will be left to chance, to frenzy? For de Kooning, in spite of the tons of control, and his sophistication to history, the answer will be Everything . . . and Nothing.

This latest ambiguity can be illustrated by a contrast of opposites. Valéry wrote in *The Esthetic Invention:*

Disorder is essential to "creation" in as much as creation defines itself as a certain "order." This creation of order relates both to *spontaneous formations,* which can be compared to those natural objects which are symmetrical or "intelligible" forms in themselves, and to the *conscious act,* where it is possible to distinguish an *end* from a *means* and to express them separately.

In a de Kooning it is impossible to distinguish the "end" from "means," or the "conscious act" from a "spontaneous formation." Sometimes paint is applied so that it runs or splatters, but it was gauged to run or splatter in that way (plate 156). The result is judged with calmness, patience, grasp, experience. The painting is observed from all sides; usually it is painted from all sides, too. Under examination it grows from the artist's experience like a spontaneous formation. It is contemplated as seen reversed in a mirror, or as if it were seen from a great distance through a reducing glass. Hazard enters in every change of angle and brushstroke. It is not unusual for a painting to be turned upside down or 90 degrees at the last minute. The artist feels he must keep off-balance in front of his work. The picture is a bet kept riding on rolls of the dice. It can be lost at any throw. When it can no longer be lost, the picture is finished. The artist is outside. And to keep his bet on the table, the most dangerous methods must be used. Peril becomes as much a part of the medium as turpentine. The means cannot be separated from the ends in the finished work (as Valéry would like to do for all Art) because the only separable means are those pounds of paint that have been scraped to the floor.

27

The action of judging the results of an act in the painting is an ethical process that, for its standards, has the intensity of the visual experience. The standard will always be flexible, as the experience is always new. Thus "the will to a system is a lack of integrity"; the fresh experience insists on its own ethical reference. A system cannot be willed. It grows out of interior forces and logic to the inevitable, unique formulation, like a crystal.

Irrelevancies of Style, including the artist's own style, must be excluded, for the experience depends, in part, upon freshness for its validity. De Kooning's *delectatio morosa* may send him back, over and over again, to shapes and hues in his own pictures, but he always uses them in explosively new contexts. If de Kooning's art is all of a piece, it is in the way a man is—my toes do not look like my hair. "Frenzy" (by which Nietzsche obviously meant pure inspiration—Wordsworth in frenzy recollected daffodils) is judged in terms of intentions. Has the act established itself as a piece of the painting? Is the "eye" an eye? Is the red the shape of "red?" The decision is based on the moment of experience and a lifetime of art, and the self-knowledge acquired of life and art and moments of experience.

The "Nothing"

BECAUSE THIS is the first attempt to view de Kooning's art as a whole, and because he frequently has been regarded as only a phenomenon of The New American Painting, it has been necessary to emphasize the methodological aspects, the "hows" of his work. From this viewpoint, it is possible to overlook that "nothing" in a painting which makes all the difference, which makes one picture great, and another ordinary.

The breadth of de Kooning's expression is extraordinary. In the early paintings of men and elliptical abstractions, there is a hushed, tragic and lyrical quality. The men gaze calmly, numbly out of the painting; sometimes their stares project triangulations of perspective into the room. Usually they are alone, lost in the intensity of their pose (the sad expressions models get when they have sat too long) or in that other intense glance—the artist looking at himself in a mirror. The rumpled jeans have stiffened forever around their thighs (in the 1930's de Kooning worked from a mannikin he had constructed, a sort of Golem in dungarees), boys are bald because hair is "impossible." Their necks and shoulders are like sacks, bursting with shapes which the artist is about to invent.

Cool aquamarines and shades of porous rose transpose the mood to abstractions of words become interiors and still-lifes. The adventure

28

is of loss and emptiness. The affirmation paradoxically comes from the lucid paint itself. The musical silver-grays of Louis Le Nain and Ingres shadow the vision.

In the early *Women,* tenderness changes to high-comedy. The *Men* are abandoned for glittering duchesses who lapse into funny poses and have a weakness for cock-eyed hats. De Kooning's Woman is of course, the White Goddess, and readers interested in her aunts are referred to archaic Boetia and the lost cities of Mycenea, Knossos and their Tara-scan settlements, to the Theban goddess Nut and Marilyn Monroe, Aztec dolls, Kali, Artemis-Isis, Willendorf, Jiggs's Maggie. But she is more interesting in herself. As the artist expands and deepens the theme, a woman in a chair, on a city street-corner, enthroned on her inside-outside porch or wharf, becomes an architecture of colonnades and domes, a landscape with a backyard on Tenth Street growing from her ocean beaches. After the initial shock of her appearance wears off, she sits next to us on a bus, or is seen waving at someone behind us in a restaurant.

The lyric gentleness left de Kooning's pictures long before the *Women* of the 1940's—although it never left altogether and returns every now and again, startling in its calm. It is replaced by a savage tearing and cutting and rending of shapes into their positions. The black-and-white abstractions at first seem to be made of chunks of people. Later the classic stability of the image becomes apparent; one can see what de Kooning meant when he said that one of them (plate 78) reminds him of seventeenth century Dutch naval prints—those pellucid bird's-eye views of tiny ships and ripples and flags with, here and there, a puff of cannon smoke moving as harmlessly over the water as a snatch of tune.

When they are first seen, the shock of de Kooning's pictures make you jump. Later their image swells in the memory, so after a few months, when you see them again, you are momentarily surprised at their actual size. The initial shock should be remembered; it is part of the esthetic response. It carries the protest of the image, and it is a rough equivalent of the ethical pressure behind it.

Ambiguity is the protean strategy that de Kooning has used to open his art so that it could become anything and everything, as paintings used to be in the past. Botticelli could play with three miles in an inch of paint. The crisis in modern art reduced the inch of paint to nothing more than 1", a disillusionment of "capabilities," as Keats used the word. De Kooning has brought miles back into the inch by inventing shapes that will switch meaning and position, jump the tracks of formalistic composition to act as background and foreground, positive

29

and negative, hot and cold, hill and thumb, letter and mouth, bird and belly. As the forms open, as the stroke becomes freer under the surer control of wider experience, colors open with concepts; the path continues to more and more wonderful diversities.

Postscript, Influences and Influence

MODERN ART, when it is good, has to be original. This is a sorry fact. We have no more artists like Petrus Christus, Botticini or Pater who were content to find a corner for their personalities and then gave their lives to the continuation of another man's innovations. Or, if such artists do exist, they feel they have to deny being subordinate. Today each painter goes through the ritual of stamping out his plot of ground, sticking a big flag in it, and declaring Independence. To be derivative means to lack character or imagination. Of course our period has not produced an army of van Eycks, Botticellis and Watteaus. The brave little proclamations of Ego often are only symptoms of a craving for passports. But in a time when originality is so necessarily prized one uncomfortable result is that the question of influence has become a taboo —like the word syphilis was a decade ago.

Before the crisis, and the categorical imperative of originality, acknowledging influence was a matter of simple courtesy. In this regard de Kooning belongs to an older European generation. He is frankly grateful to the artists who have taught him things he could use, and he considers influence to be the healthy, indeed prerequisite, condition for the existence of art.

His influences have been: Picasso and Cubism; through Picasso, Ingres; through Cubism the comportment of Duchamp; and Kandinsky, Miró, Gorky. It is a question of learning, not a matter of hints—although hints are important, too. The hint about introducing letters into abstractions, for example, surely came from Miró, Cubist collages and Stuart Davis. Certain poses (the Bertin squat) come from Ingres, as does a courtly habit of draftsmanship, a dedication to drawing, a quality of grays. Picasso obviously influenced the early *Men* and *Women*. Some rounded abstract shapes echo Miró. Matisse, Picasso and Ingres make explicit the theme of sexuality which is a major part of de Kooning's painting. Art history enters, too; Rembrandt and Hals, Rubens and Brueghel, van Gogh, Leonardo, Giotto ...

The problem becomes slightly complicated with the influence of Arshile Gorky. There was an interaction between Gorky and de Kooning which de Kooning has gone to some lengths to contradict, insisting, "he influenced me." At any event, Picasso and Ingres probably were seen by de Kooning from Gorky's viewpoint, and some of de Kooning's *Men* of the 1930's are very close to Gorky's self-portraits. One difference is that de Kooning worked from mirrors, Gorky from photographs.

De Kooning went off on his own, freely discovering for himself hundreds of paintings, treating art history as an available part of culture. He has been interested in Mondrian as a personality and has perceived the flashes of light at the intersections of Mondrian's paintings—and the metaphysical flashes in van Gogh. You can find Soutine (of the Ceret period), Courbet, Lautrec and the Le Nains and Pompeian frescoes in de Kooning's pictures. In his latitude, art breathes art.

The question of de Kooning's enormous effect on other artists is more difficult to discuss. By the mid-1950's he had become the most influential artist at work in the world, and by and large his influence was a beneficial one. His form was "open," his ideas could be used profitably and intelligently. Pollock's black-on-white heads of 1951 obviously were done with an eye cocked at de Kooning's *Women*. Franz Kline's black-and-white paintings of 1950, as well as those of Esteban Vicente, were painted after direct contact with de Kooning's abstractions of 1948–49. Elaine de Kooning, Marca-Relli, Resnick and Tworkov also learned from his example. These were all intimates. Probably there was interaction. At any event, each quickly went off to establish his own standards. But there is no doubt that de Kooning acted as a decisive leader in the formative years that saw the appearance of new kinds of painting in New York. His influence is also seen (and has been acknowledged) in works by Joan Mitchell, Larry Rivers, Alfred Leslie, Grace Hartigan, Fairfield Porter, Michael Goldberg . . .

As de Kooning's influence spread, it was diluted. Today young painters blow-up enormous pictures after a glimpse of small de Kooning sketches; whole one-man shows have been fabricated from a half-finished "original." Many European artists base their pictures on reproductions from magazines and newspapers. It has become a comedy of mannerisms.

Free of these recent encumbrances (which only confuse that part of the public for whom the image of de Kooning's work is distorted by exposure to its half-understood by-products), the artist's latest pictures stand as immanent "chunks of vista dumped into a room." At the mid-point in his career, de Kooning, fifty-five-years-old, seems to be closing-off his image. There may be little room for any one else to work in between his idea and his act. And as the image becomes less available to other artists, it grows ever more open. It is more receptive to new experiences, to the fresh wind from the ocean or to the calmer breeze that hovers over the "bums who lie poisoned in vast delivery portals" (whom he had watched with Denby in the 1930's); a bet on death and on what is living—alive, growing, open . . .

NOTES ON THE PLATES

De Kooning's pictures are worked on over and over again during long periods of time. He did not sell paintings with any regularity until 1954. Old pictures in the studio often were painted out, or drastically changed. He does not sign pictures until they leave the studio. He almost never dates them, and in the case of the few dated paintings and drawings, the dates usually refer to when the picture was sold or given away to a friend—which might have been several years after completion.

This has made the chronology of de Kooning's work a problem of interior stylistic examination, but this was enormously helped by the artist who was able to give several firm pegs from which other dates could hang (e.g., plate 9, done the summer he went to Woodstock, plate 82, at Black Mountain, etc.), and to indicate which pictures were in which exhibitions (e.g., plates 24 and 45, shown at the Bignou Gallery, Feb. 1943). However, aside from a handful of works, most can be dated only within 18 to 24 months. And a few may be off by 36. The author hopes to correct any serious lapses in a longer book on the artist which is planned for publication in about two years.

Where dimensions are not given, the work was unavailable within the deadlines set by this publication. This, too, will be corrected in the forthcoming book.

Museum credits: Plate 92, given to Vassar by Mrs. Richard Deutsch, Greenwich, Conn. Plate 102 and 123, given to the Nelson Gallery by William Inge, N.Y. Plate 108, bought by the Art Institute through its Logan Purchase Prize and gifts from Mr. and Mrs. Noah Goldowsky, Glenco, Ill., and Edgar Kaufmann, Jr., N.Y. Plate 121, given to the Museum of Modern Art by Mrs. John D. Rockefeller, III, N.Y. Plate 127, F.M. Hall Collection of Nebraska University. Plate 135, given to the Brooklyn Museum by Mr. and Mrs. A. Bradley Martin, Glen Head, L.I. Plate 141, Seymour Knox Collection, Albright Art Gallery, Buffalo, N.Y.

ADDITIONS AND CORRECTIONS

Plate 6 is a horizontal painting; the top is along the binding edge.
Plate 12 is titled *September Morn.*
Plate 16 is titled *Merritt Parkway.*
Plate 55, *Nude,* dates from ca. 1936.
Plate 77 is owned by I. M. Pei.

1. Painting. 1959. Oil, 62¾ x 49½″. Sidney Janis Gallery. Photographed a few weeks after completion, March, 1959, when still untitled

2. TOP: *Forest of Zogbaum*. 1958. Oil, 48 x 59″. Sidney Janis Gallery
3. BOTTOM: *Duck Pond*. 1958. Oil, 48 x 59″. Sidney Janis Gallery

Montauk Highway. 1958. Oil, 59 x 48″. Sidney Janis Gallery

5. Painting. 1959. Oil, 80 x 70⅛". Sidney Janis Gallery. Photographed a few weeks after completion, March, 1959, when still untitled

6. Untitled abstraction. Ca. 1931. Oil, 23⅞ x 33″. Collection the artist

7. TOP: Untitled painting. Ca. 1928. Oil. Collection Elaine de Kooning
8. BOTTOM: *Death of a Man*, detail. Ca. 1932. Now destroyed

9. TOP: Still-life. Ca. 1929. Oil, 48 x 24″. Collection
   Milton Robertson
10. BOTTOM: Still-life. Ca. 1929. Oil, 32⅛ x 24″.
    Collection the artist

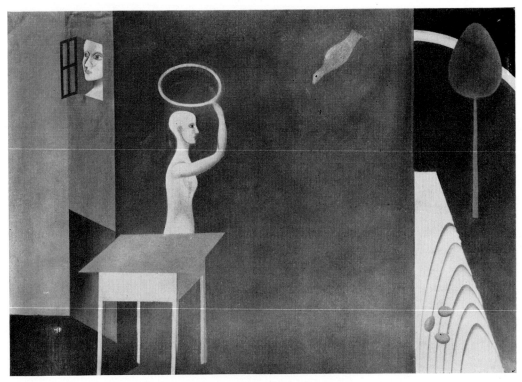

11. TOP: Untitled painting. Ca. 1934. Oil. Collection John Becker
12. BOTTOM: Untitled painting. Ca. 1931. Oil. Now destroyed

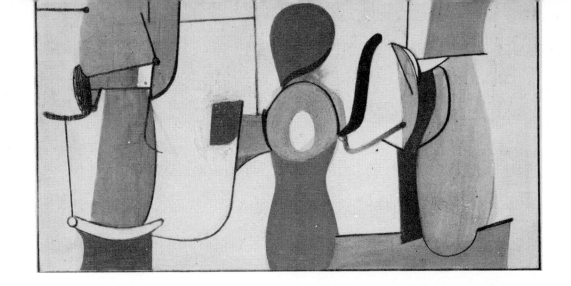

13. TOP: Study for Williamsburg Housing Project (W.P.A.). 1935.
14. MIDDLE: Model for mural for French Line Pier (W.P.A., under Léger). 1935.
15. BOTTOM: Design for N. Y. World's Fair mural for Hall of Pharmacy. 1937.
    Present location of the three unknown

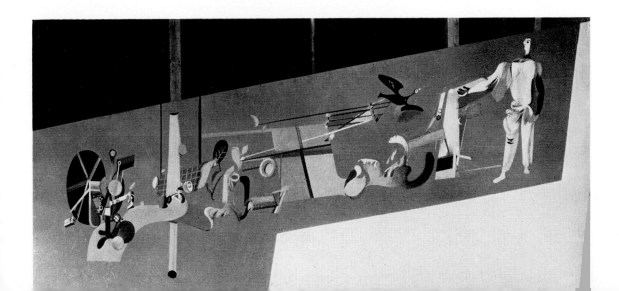

16. TOP: *Self-Portrait with Imaginary Brother.* Ca. 1938. Pencil drawing, 12 x 10″. Collection Saul Steinberg
17. BOTTOM: *Two Men Standing.* Ca. 1938. Oil, 60 x 44″. Private collection, N. Y.

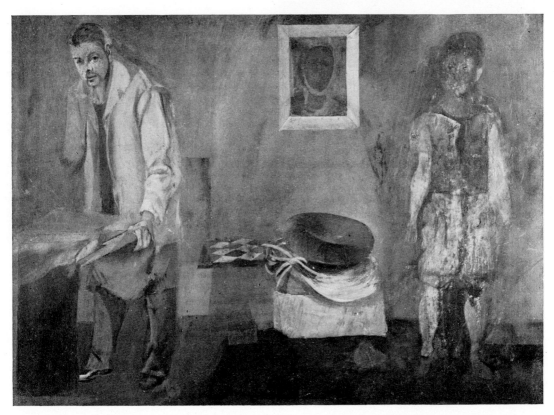

18. TOP LEFT: *Working Man.* Ca. 1938. Pencil drawing, 11 x 9″. Collection Max Margulis
19. TOP RIGHT: *Seated Man.* Ca. 1938. Oil. Now destroyed
20. BOTTOM: Untitled painting. Ca. 1937. Oil on board, 13½ x 19″. Collection Edwin Denby—
    Rudolph Burckhardt

21. LEFT: Drawing for *Seated Man*. Ca. 1939. Pencil on paper, on
sheet 14½ x 9½". Collection the artist
22. RIGHT: *Seated Man*. Ca. 1939. Oil, 38 x 34". Collection the artist

23. *Man.* Ca. 1939. Oil on paper, 11 x 10″. Collection Edwin Denby—Rudolph Burckhardt

24. TOP: *Elaine de Kooning*. Ca.
1940. Pencil on paper. Collection
Mr. and Mrs. Daniel Brustlein
25. BOTTOM: Drawing for a commissioned portrait. Ca. 1940. Pencil
on paper, 16½ x 11″. Collection
the artist

26. LEFT: *Portrait of Max Margulis*. Ca. 1944.
Oil on board, 46 x 28″. Collection Max
Margulis

27. RIGHT: Drawing of Max Margulis. Ca. 1944.
Pencil on paper, 12½ x 9½″. Collection Max
Margulis

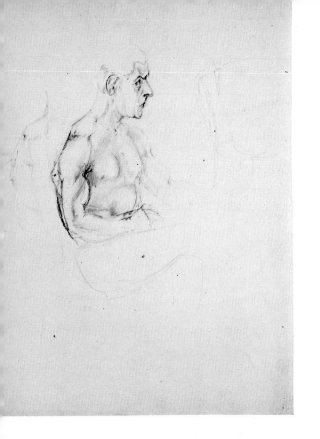

28–31. Four drawings for *Glazier*. Ca. 1940. Pencil on paper, 14 x 11″. Collection the artist

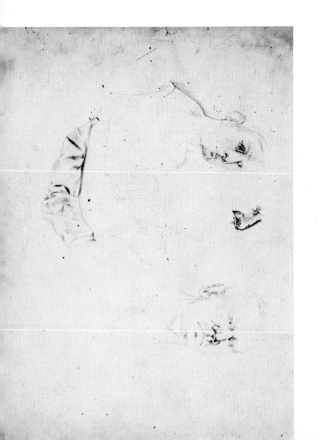

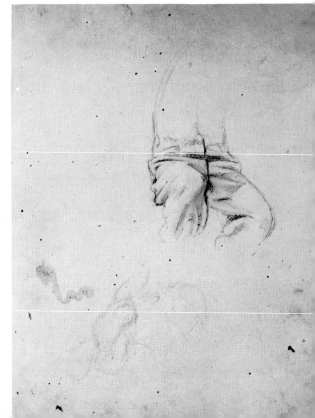

32. *Glazier*. Ca. 1940. Oil, 54 x 44″. Private collection, N. Y.

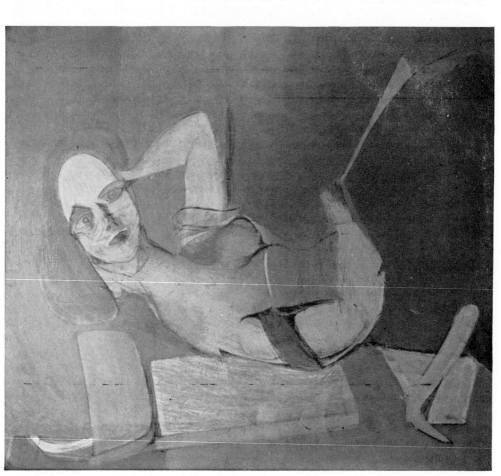

33. LEFT: *Woman Sitting*. Ca. 1939. Oil on board, 48 x 42″. Collection Mr. and Mrs. Daniel Brustlein
34. RIGHT: *Seated Woman*. Ca. 1940. Oil on board, 54 ½ x 36″. Collection Mr. and Mrs. Albert M. Greenfield

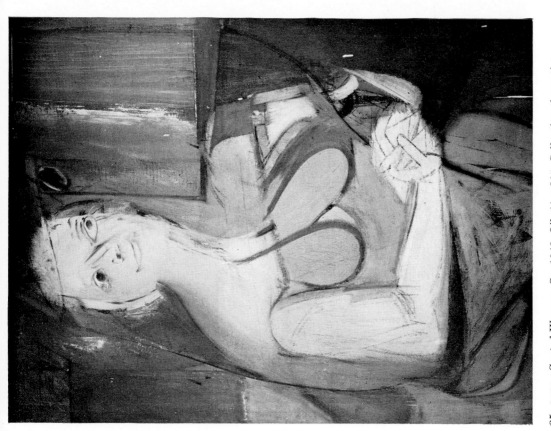

35. LEFT: *Seated Woman.* Ca. 1942. Oil, 41 x 30″. Collection the artist
36. RIGHT: *Woman.* Ca. 1943. Oil, 46 x 32″. Collection Edwin Denby —Rudolph Burckhardt

37. *Pink Lady.* Ca. 1944. Oil, 48¼ x 35¼". Collection Fairfield Porter

38. LEFT: Unfinished portrait of Rudolph
    Burckhardt (detail below). Ca. 1939.
    Oil. Collection Edwin Denby—Ru-
    dolph Burckhardt
39. RIGHT: *Seated Figure ("Classic
    Male")*. Ca. 1940. Oil on board, 54½ x
    36". Collection Mrs. Robert Leonhardt

40. LEFT: *Standing Man.* Ca. 1942. Oil. Collection Charles Rieger.   41. RIGHT: *Acrobat.* Ca. 1942. Oil, 36½ x 25½". Private collection, N. Y.

42. LEFT: *Woman.* Ca. 1942. Oil. Now destroyed.   43. RIGHT: *Woman.* Ca. 1942. Oil. Now destroyed

44. *Nude.* Ca. 1940. Pencil on paper. 10½ x 13". Collection the artist

45. *Elegy*. Ca. 1939. Oil, 24 x 36″. Collection Helena Rubinstein

46. TOP: Untitled painting. Ca. 1937. Oil on paper, 10 x 14″. Collection Elaine de Kooning
47. BOTTOM: Untitled painting. Ca. 1938. Oil on paper, 25 x 30″. Collection Mr. and Mrs. Daniel Brustlein

48. TOP: Untitled painting. Ca. 1938. Oil on board, 9½ x 15″. Collection Walter Auerbach
49. BOTTOM: Untitled pen drawing. Ca. 1938. Ink on board, 9 x 9½″. Collection
Elaine de Kooning

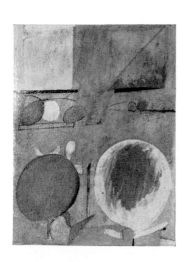

50. TOP LEFT: Untitled painting. Ca. 1938. Oil on board, 11 x 9½″. Collection Edwin Denby—Rudolph Burckhardt

51. TOP RIGHT: Unfinished painting. Ca. 1940. Oil, 37 x 34″. Collection Edwin Denby—Rudolph Burckhardt

52. BOTTOM LEFT: Untitled painting. Ca. 1938. Oil on paper, 4 x 3¼″. Collection Edwin Denby—Rudolph Burckhardt

53. BOTTOM RIGHT: Untitled painting. Ca. 1939. Oil. Collection Frank K. Safford, Jr., or Denby—Burckhardt

54. TOP: *The Wave*. Ca. 1942. Oil, 48 x 48″. Present location unknown
55. BOTTOM: Untitled painting. Ca. 1942, Oil, 46 x 46″. Collection
Edwin Denby—Rudolph Burckhardt

56. TOP: Untitled painting *("Match-book")*. Ca. 1942. Oil on paper. Collection Marjorie Luyckx
57. BOTTOM: Untitled painting. Ca. 1944. Oil, 13½ x 21¼". Collection Fairfield Porter

58. TOP: Untitled painting. Ca. 1943. Oil. Collection Frank O'Hara
59. BOTTOM: Untitled painting. Ca. 1943. Oil on paper. Collection Alexander Bing

60. *Pink Angels.* Ca. 1945. Oil, 52 x 40″. Collection Jeanne Reynal

61. LEFT: *The Marshes*. Ca. 1945. Oil on board, 33½ x 23¼″. Sidney Janis Gallery
62. TOP: Study for a backdrop for a dance recital. Ca. 1946. Oil on paper. Collection Edwin Denby—Rudolph Burckhardt
63. RIGHT: Sketch for Backdrop. Ca. 1946. Pastel, 9¾ x 10″. Collection Donald Blinken

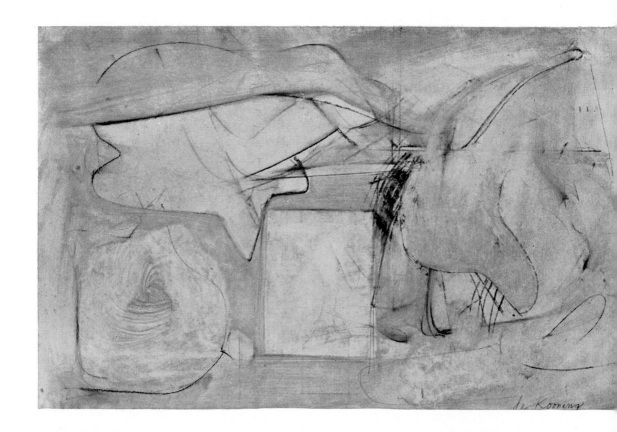

64. TOP: Untitled painting. Ca. 1946. Oil on paper. Collection Mr. and Mrs. Daniel Brustlein
65. BOTTOM: Untitled painting. Ca. 1946. Oil on paper, 27½ x 34¼". Collection Noah Goldowsky

66. TOP: *Brown and White.* Ca. 1947. Oil on paper, 24 x 36″. Ex-collection Dr. Jack Greenbaum
67. BOTTOM: *Fire Island.* Ca. 1947. Oil on paper, 19 x 26½″. Collection Gov. and Mrs. Nelson Rockefeller

68. *Light in August*. Ca. 1946. Oil and enamel on paper, 55 x 42″. Collection Elizabeth Duhrssen

69. TOP: *Open Road*. Ca. 1948. Oil on paper, 30 x 40″. Collection Mr. and Mrs. Albert M. Greenfield
70. BOTTOM: *The Netherlands*. Container Corporation commission. January, 1945. 10½ x 8½″. Container Corporation

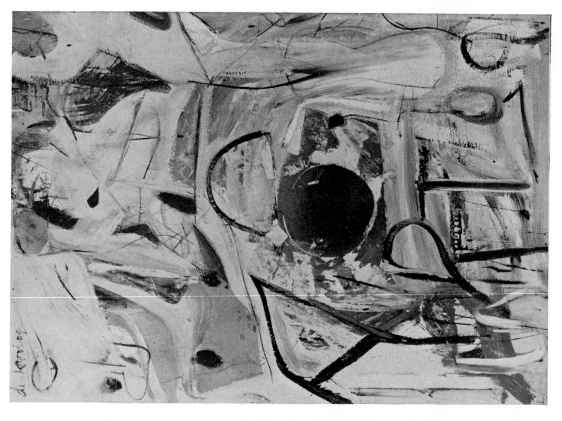

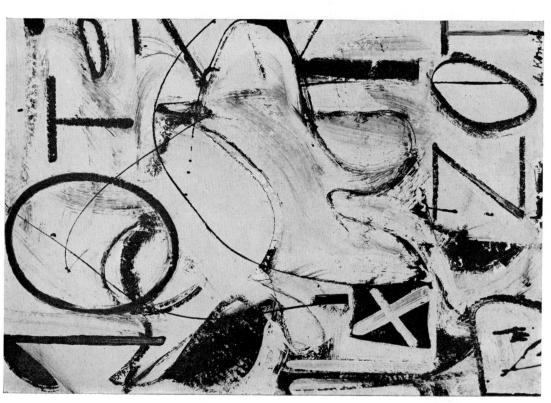

71. LEFT: *Zurich*. 1947. Oil on paper, 36¼ x 24¼". Collection Herbert Ferber
72. RIGHT: *Noon*. 1947. Oil on paper, 42 x 22¼". Collection M

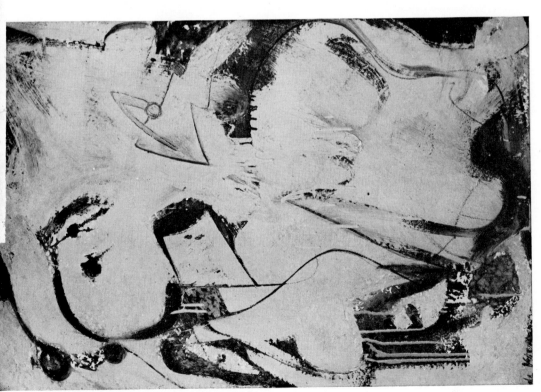

73. LEFT: *The Moraine.* 1947. Oil on paper, 35½ x 23¾". Collection Mrs. Culver Orswell
74. RIGHT: *Valentine.* 1947. Oil on paper, 36 x 24". Collection Al Lazar

75. TOP: *Mailbox*. 1947. Oil on paper, 23¼ x 30". Collection Gov. and Mrs. Nelson Rockefeller
76. BOTTOM: *"Orestes."* 1947. Enamel on paper, 24 x 30". Collection Mr. and Mrs. John Stephan

77. TOP: *Painting*. 1948. Enamel on paper, 42½ x 56″. The Museum of Modern Art
78. BOTTOM: Untitled painting. 1948. Enamel on paper, 29½ x 40″. Private collection, N. Y.

79. TOP: *Dark Pond*. 1948. Enamel on paper. Collection Jeanne Reynal
80. BOTTOM: *Night Square*. 1948. Enamel on paper, 30 x 40". Collection Martha Jackson

81. TOP LEFT: Untitled painting, dated 1947. Oil on board, 30 x 22½″. Collection Elinor Poindexter
82. TOP RIGHT: *Stenographer*. 1948. Oil on paper. Collection Al Lazar
83. BOTTOM LEFT: *January*. 1948. Oil on paper, 18¾ x 15½″. Collection Vincent Melzac
84. BOTTOM RIGHT: Untitled painting. 1948. Oil on paper. Collection Al Lazar

85. LEFT: Untitled woman. Ca. 1948. Oil on paper, 14 x 11". Collection Elinor Poindexter
86. RIGHT: Untitled woman. Ca. 1947. Present location unknown

87. LEFT: *Woman*. Ca. 1949. Oil, 64 x 46″. University of North Carolina
88. RIGHT: *Woman*. Ca. 1949. Oil, 60 x 48″. Mr. and Mrs. Boris Leavitt

89. LEFT: Untitled painting. Ca. 1947. Oil on paper. Collection Al Lazar
90. RIGHT: Untitled painting. Ca. 1947. Oil on paper. Collection Al Lazar

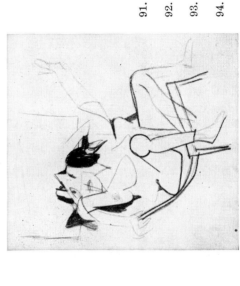

91. TOP LEFT: Pencil drawing on paper. Ca. 1947.
    10¾″ high. Collection the artist
92. TOP RIGHT: Untitled painting. Ca. 1948. Oil on
    paper, 21 x 32″. Vassar College
93. BOTTOM LEFT: *Pink Lady*. Ca. 1948. Oil on paper,
    18½ x 18½″. Collection Donald Blinken
94. BOTTOM RIGHT: Pencil drawing on cardboard. Ca.
    1948. 11½ x 9½″. Collection the artist

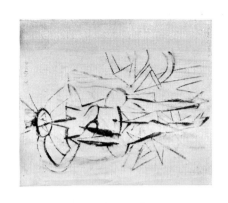

95. LEFT: *Black Friday.* 1949. Oil on paper, 30 x 40". Collection Mrs. H. Gates Lloyd
96. RIGHT: Untitled painting. Ca. 1949. Oil on paper. Collection Harold Rosenberg

97. *Ashville.* 1948–49. Oil on paper. Phillips Gallery, Washington

 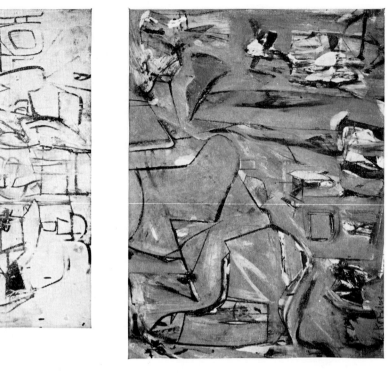

98. TOP LEFT: Untitled painting. Ca. 1948. Oil on paper. Present location unknown
99. BOTTOM LEFT: Untitled painting. Ca. 1948. Oil on paper. Present location unknown
100. TOP RIGHT: *Black Friday*. 1949. Oil on paper, 30 x 40". Collection Mrs. H. Gates Lloyd
101. BOTTOM RIGHT: *Gansevoort Street*. Ca. 1949. Oil on board, 20 x 40". Collection Gov. and Mrs. Nelson Rockefeller

102. TOP LEFT: *Warehouse Mannequins.* Ca. 1949. Oil on paper, 24 x 34½". Collection Mr. and Mrs. C. B. Wright
103. BOTTOM LEFT: *Boudoir.* Ca. 1950. Oil on paper, 27½ x 33¼". William Rockhill Nelson Gallery
104. TOP RIGHT: *Sailcloth.* Ca. 1949. Oil on paper, 26¾ x 31¾". Collection Mr. and Mrs. M. H. Grossman
105. BOTTOM RIGHT: *Boudoir.* Ca. 1950. Oil on paper, 14½ x 20¾". Collection Mr. and Mrs. Kenneth Tishler

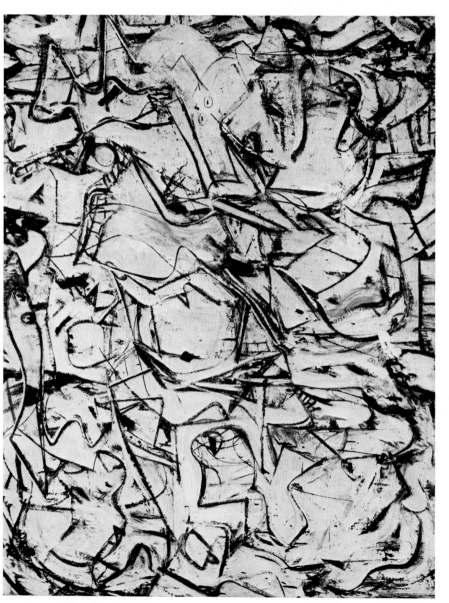

106. LEFT: *Attic*. 1949. Oil, 61½ x 80". Collection Mrs. Albert Newman
107. RIGHT: *Little Attic*. Ca. 1949. Oil on paper, 30½ x 40". Collection Dr. Israel Rosen

108. *Excavation*. 1950. Oil, 80⅛ x 100⅛". The Art Institute of Chicago

109. LEFT: *Two Standing Women.* Ca. 1949. Oil on paper. Collection Larry Aldrich
110. RIGHT: *Two Women on a Wharf.* 1949. Oil on paper and pasted paper, 24¾ x 24¾". Collection Edward F. Dragon

111. LEFT: *Woman I*, stage 1. Summer, 1950 112. RIGHT: *Woman I*, stage 2. 1950

112. THE WAVE. Summer, 1959. Pastel. 19 3/4" x 25". The Art Institute of Chicago

114. LEFT: *Woman I*, stage 3. 1951   115. RIGHT: *Woman I*, stage 4. 1951

116. LEFT: *Woman I*, stage 5. 1951-52 117. RIGHT: *Woman I*, stage 6. 1951-52

118. LEFT: Drawings for *Woman I*, detail. Charcoal on paper of skirt and face. Now destroyed
119. RIGHT: Charcoal drawing for *Woman I*. 1951-52. 14 x 11". Collection William Inge

120. *Woman I*. 1952. Oil, 76 x 58″. The Museum of Modern Art

121. TOP LEFT: *Woman II*. 1952–53. Oil, 58 x 43". The Museum of Modern Art
122. BOTTOM LEFT: *Woman III*. 1952–53. Oil, 67 x 48". Collection Frances Pernas
123. RIGHT: *Woman IV*. 1952–53. Oil, 59 x 46¼". William Rockhill Nelson Gallery

124. LEFT: *Woman V*. 1952-53. Oil, 61 x 45″. Collection Mrs. Maurice Culberg
125. RIGHT: *Woman, Ocher*. 1954-55. Oil, 40 x 30″. Collection Mrs. Edwin S. Gallagher

126. LEFT: *Woman and Bicycle.* 1953. Oil, 76½ x 49″. Whitney Museum of American Art
127. RIGHT: *Woman.* 1954. Oil on paper, 25¾ x 19½″. University of Nebraska

128. ABOVE: *Woman VI*. 1953. Oil, 69 x 60". Carnegie Institute, Pittsburgh
129. FACING PAGE: Detail of *Woman VI*

130. TOP: *Two Women*. 1953. Oil on paper, 22½ x 28½". Collection J. Benjamin Townsend
131. BOTTOM: *Two Women*. 1952. Charcoal drawing, 22 x 29". Collection Mrs. Leo Castelli

132. TOP: *Two Women*. 1953. Pencil drawing, 18 x 24". Collection the artist
133. MIDDLE: *Three Women*. 1953-54. Pencil drawing, 10 x 26". Collection the artist
134. BELOW: *Two Women*. 1954. Pencil drawing, 12½ x 20½". Collection the artist

135. TOP LEFT: *Woman.* 1953–54. Oil on paper, 35½ x 23½". In The Brooklyn Museum Collection
136. TOP RIGHT: *Woman.* 1954. Charcoal drawing. Collection Harold Rosenberg
137. BOTTOM LEFT: *Woman (Green).* 1945–55. Oil, 30 x 23". Collection Mr. and Mrs. Milton Gordon
138. BOTTOM RIGHT: *Woman as Landscape.* 1955. Oil, 45½ x 41". Collection Martha Jackson

139. Untitled abstraction. 1955. Oil, 79 x 69″. The Solomon R. Guggenheim Museum

140. TOP: *Police Gazette*. 1954-55. Oil, 34 x 50″. Collection Walter Bareiss
141. BOTTOM: *Gotham News*. 1955-56. Oil 69 x 79″. Albright Art Gallery

142. TOP: *Saturday Night*. 1955-56. Oil, 69 x 79″. Washington University
143. BOTTOM: *Street Corner Incident*. 1955. Oil, 41 x 48½″. Collection Barney Rosset

144. *Interchange*. 1955. Oil, 79 x 69". Collection Edgar Kaufmann, Jr.

145. *Easter Monday.* 1956. Oil, 96 x 74″. The Metropolitan Museum of Art

146. TOP: *Sagamore*. 1955. Oil, 22½ x 27½″. Collection E. A. Navaretta
147. BOTTOM: *The Time of the Fire*. 1956. Oil, 59 x 80″. Collection Dr. Israel Rosen

148. TOP: *July*. 1956. Oil, 68½ x 79″. Collection Mrs. Culver Orswell
149. BOTTOM: *Backyard on Tenth Street*. 1956. Oil, 48 x 58½″. The Baltimore Museum of Art

150. *First of January*. 1956. Oil, 78 x 68½". Collection Dr. and Mrs. John A. Cook

151. ABOVE: Portrait of Jack Greenbaum. Ca. 1956. Oil, 50 x 34". Collection Dr. Jack Greenbaum
152. FACING PAGE: Photograph of Dr. Greenbaum and his portrait

153. *Bolton Landing.* 1957. Oil, 83¾ x 74″. Inland Steel Company

154. TOP: *Leaves in Weehawken*. 1958. Oil, 48 x 59". Collection I. D. Grossman
155. BOTTOM: Untitled painting. 1959. Oil, 49½ x 62¾". Sidney Janis Gallery

156. LEFT: *February 1957*, detail. Oil, 79 x 69″. Sidney Janis Gallery
157. RIGHT: *February 1957*

CHRONOLOGY

THE ARTIST was born in Rotterdam, April 24, 1904. His mother, Cornelia Nobel de Kooning, still lives in Holland. His father, Leendert de Kooning, was a distributor of wines, beers and soft-drinks.

In 1916 he left grammar school to work as an apprentice to Jan and Jaap Gidding, who ran a firm of commercial artists and decorators. At Jaap Gidding's advice, he enrolled for the full course of evening classes at the Academie voor Beeldende Kunsten en Technische Wetenschappen, where, for the next eight years, he received instruction in the fine and applied arts. There was no formal graduation or certification for artists (as, on the other hand, there was for plumbers) from the Academy. Students remained there until it was felt that they could practice their crafts and techniques competently. Emphasis was placed on a thorough knowledge of the classical disciplines (drawing, anatomy, perspective, color theory) and accepted methods (architectural rendering, wood-graining, lettering, etc.). The atmosphere was lively. (He remembers working with Mies, and the director, Heiberg.)

In 1920 he left the Giddings' establishment to work under Bernard Romein, an artist who also had the post of directing the painting of signs and making of displays for a large department store. Romein had a wide comprehension of the arts of the past and a deep sympathy for the vanguards of the present. Thus while de Kooning was keeping up his work at the Academy, he was also being introduced to the aims and accomplishments of the brilliant *de Stijl* group then flourishing in Holland (under the leadership of Mondrian and van Doesburg), to the Paris moderns, to Frank Lloyd Wright, the poetry of Whitman. This was a direct contact with the revolutionary ferment that has marked the youthful phases of modern art in all its best periods. A teacher at the Academy, Jongert, also encouraged de Kooning's interest in the radical art of the time.

De Kooning, of course, was attracted to other contemporary Dutch manifestations—to the local versions of Art Nouveau, which dominated much of the current commercial art, to the paintings of Toorop, van Konijnenburg, van Dongen —as well as to the Italian Pointillist Segantini, Millet and the Barbizon School.

In 1924, de Kooning and some friends went to Belgium. He continued painting and took odd jobs with decorators' firms. He saw, but was not particularly influenced by, contemporary Belgian Expressionists, and attended classes in Brussels and Antwerp. In 1925, he returned to Rotterdam and the classes at the Academy.

In 1926, he sailed to America, and quickly was pleased by the appearance of New York and its suburbs and by the freer atmosphere—compared to the more compressed environment of the Lowlands. (He spoke almost no English, and once remarked jokingly to an interviewer that "the only word I knew was 'Yes' "; a crack that has been quoted deadpan since in several articles.)

At first he supported himself by housepainting, making Hoboken, N.J. a base of operations. But a year later he moved across the river to Manhattan and a studio on Forty-second Street. He took commercial-art jobs—working for decorators, briefly for the department store of A.S. Beck, and doing murals for speakeasies (Anton Refregier, who worked "for gangsters" with de Kooning on some of these murals, remembers that most of the "gangsters didn't like modern art"). He also found time to visit museums and galleries and to pursue his own ideas of painting. Some small pictures of around 1928 indicate he was experimenting with abstraction at this time, some of it symbolic, some influenced by the flat colored geometries of Kandinsky.

In 1927, at a gallery, he met the painter and connoisseur John Graham, who became one of the first to recognize de Kooning's exceptional gifts. Through another painter, Mischa Resnikoff, he met Arshile Gorky.

Gorky and de Kooning became close friends, sharing a studio for a number of years in the late 1930's and mutually helping and influencing each other. Gorky was more sophisticated to what was happening at the moment in modern art, de Kooning had a more sophisticated knowledge of the artist's means. Gorky was certainly more flamboyant as a public personality in the art world, and for a number of years de Kooning was considered his follower. Comparison of their paintings of the same periods indicates that a vital and sharp interaction existed between the two painters, sometimes approaching the Picasso-Braque closeness of relationship, but usually the works are a good deal further apart.

Shortly after Gorky's tragic death, de Kooning affirmed his debt to his friend in a public letter [see Bibliography].

In 1928, he spent some summer months in the artists' colony of Woodstock, N. Y. A few semi-abstract paintings of this period still exist.

Around 1934, de Kooning met the poet Edwin Denby, who became the first systematic collector of his paintings. Through Denby he became friends with the photographer-painter Rudolph Burckhardt (who took almost all the photographs of early paintings by the artist that are reproduced in this book) and many composers and performing artists in the fields of music and the ballet, including Virgil Thompson, Aaron Copeland, Paul Bowles, David Diamond.

In 1935, de Kooning spent a year on the Federal Arts Project—the first time that he was able to paint full-time, and he has painted full-time ever since.

One of his assignments was to work on projects for a mural for the Williamsburg Federal Housing Project (the murals themselves were never executed). A sketch 20 by 14 inches, for a panel (14½ feet high, 9½ feet wide) was shown in 1936 in the Museum of Modern Art's exhibition of work done under government auspices; also included in this exhibition were many of the artists de Kooning knew at the time: Gorky, Stuart Davis, leader of the abstract contingent in New York,

114

and Ilya Bolotowsky, Byron Browne, Francis Criss, Balcomb Greene, Jan Matulka, George McNeil [see Bibliography 17]. De Kooning also worked under the eminent French Cubist Fernand Léger on a mural commission for the French Lines' pier.

In 1937, he was commissioned to submit designs for a mural for the New York World's Fair, *Medecine,* for the Hall of Pharmacy. His sketch was accepted, and the composition applied to the huge curved walls by professional muralists. It was a three-part mural, Michael Loew had part "A," de Kooning part "B," and Stuyvesant van Veen "C." Loew described "B" in the project [see Bibliography] as "92 feet long, 29 feet high . . . concerned to give a multicolored effect on a white background . . . depicted in more traditional, allegorical terms."

In de Kooning's biographical sketch prepared by the Fair's publicity department the following is listed: "State Academy Award, Rotterdam; Silver Medal, Academy of Plastic Arts; Member American Abstract Artists; Artists Union; Mural Artists Guild (Local 829 A.F. of L. affiliate, now in process of formation); Murals and Interiors: Residence of Norman K. Winston, Vladimir and Matty Erlington; Williamsburg Housing Project, New York City Housing Authority; American Music Hall Night Club (associate painter); New French Line Pier Sketches, New York City Department of Docks, associated with Léger."

In the mid-1930's, de Kooning was painting highly original abstractions in grayed colors with pink or green accents glittering among the circumscribed forms; and also series of figure pieces in meticulous, formal realism. Both these styles advanced for the next decade, becoming refined and complicated in the advancement. In the late 1930's, he was visited in his studio by Clement Greenberg. In their subsequent conversations de Kooning's ideas had a profound influence on the future art-critic.

A perceptive and touching account of de Kooning and New York artists in the 1930's has been written by Edwin Denby [see Bibliography, 38].

Although always reluctant to exhibit, wanting to solve problems which endlessly became endlessly more difficult, de Kooning did show a few pictures in group exhibitions in the early 1940's. A complete list of these appearances, as well as of his later one-man exhibitions and joint exhibitions appears in the Bibliography.

In 1943 he married an art student, Elaine Fried; today she is a well-known painter and writer on art.

By the mid 1940's, de Kooning was famous among New York artists; his work had become widely influential and highly appreciated in the limited circle of the art world. At this time, however, American collectors and museums concentrated, almost entirely, either on European art or local Social Realism. The difficulties in being an artist in New York in the 1930's and 1940's—and, for many, in the 1950's —were (and are) tremendous. In the catalogue of the 1930's exhibition [Bibliography 38], Gorky's wife, Agnes Phillips, wrote:

Gorky described [the 1930's] as the bleakest, most spirit-crushing period of his life and spoke with bitterness of the futility of such paralyzing poverty for the artist . . . He often said that, if a human being managed to emerge from such a period, it could not be as a whole man and that there was no recovery from the blows and wounds of such a struggle to survive.

De Kooning, of course, jokes about the difficulties of these days. And Edwin Denby wrote:

At one party [at de Kooning's studio] the talk turned to the condition of the painter in America, the bitterness and unfairness of his poverty and disregard. People had a great deal to say on the subject, and they said it, but the talk ended in gloomy silence. In the pause, Gorky's deep voice came from under a table, "Nineteen miserable years have I lived in America." Everybody burst out laughing.

By 1946, de Kooning had embarked on a series of black-and-white abstractions, many of them done in commercial enamel paints; he never used colored house-paints in his pictures as he felt these might not be permanent. One of the reasons for this turn to monochrome paintings is that the artist could not afford a plentiful supply of tube colors. These were shown in his first one-man exhibition in New York at the Egan Gallery [see Bibliography 1 and reviews]. It immediately established him as an artist of major stature in America and internationally—for American art was becoming international.

Painters such as Arshile Gorky, Jackson Pollock, Mark Rothko, Adolph Gottlieb, Hans Hofmann, William Baziotes, Clyfford Still, Robert Motherwell—de Kooning had close associations with most of them—were emerging as the most dynamic painters of the postwar period. De Kooning now became a leader of this moment (for it was neither a movement nor a school), and although collectors in America still were addicted to Dufy or Utrillo, his works were prominently exhibited in leading museums—the Whitney, the Museum of Modern Art, the Art Institute of Chicago, and so forth.

In the summer of 1948, de Kooning taught at Black Mountain College, then headed by Josef Albers. There he renewed his acquaintanceship with Buckminster Fuller, designer and engineer of the Dymaxion, and with the composer John Cage.

In the scholastic year 1950–51, he commuted to New Haven to teach at the Yale Art School—also headed, at this time, by Albers. His second one-man exhibition was held in April 1951 at the Egan Gallery. It included a number of abstractions keyed to pale reds and yellow, but by this time de Kooning had already returned to the theme of the figure. His largest abstract painting, *Excavation* (which in November 1951 would win the first prize at the Chicago Art Institute annual; see Bibliography 28), was taken from his studio to be shipped to the Biennale, Venice [Bibliography 11], in June 1950. A few days later he began to work on a large painting, *Woman I,* which would not be finished until the summer of 1952.

The second one-man show had a critical success. Almost no pictures were sold from it.

For eighteen months de Kooning worked on the big canvas of *Woman I,* scraping away version after version. Early in 1952, just as it seemed to approach completion, it was abandoned as "impossible." In the spring of that year, he showed it to the art historian Meyer Schapiro and suddenly saw a way to finish it, and with it a series of other oils on the theme.

Later that summer he spent a few months in the Hamptons, Long Island, a popular vacation site for New York artists and writers, to which he has gone frequently since. A series of pastels, many of two women, were done in these months.

116

Oils and pastels of Women were exhibited at the Janis Gallery in March 1953.

The Women made a traumatic impression on the public—to date, they have been the last modern paintings to do so [see Bibliography 4 and reviews]. The Museum of Modern Art, New York, bought *Woman I*, which has since become the most widely reproduced painting of the 1950's in the world.

Because de Kooning was so closely associated with what was being called "the modern American school," his earlier works were largely forgotten. They were seen in retrospectives in Boston [see Bibliography 5] and Venice [see Bibliography 14] and in group exhibitions, but they often were dismissed as the early heresies of a "convert" to abstraction.

De Kooning continued to paint the Women series for about eighteen months. They were still all but unsaleable in 1955. A New York dealer, Martha Jackson, bought a number of his paintings and drawings and exhibited them in November of that year [see Bibliography 6 and reviews].

In the summer of 1955, the Women began to turn into abstractions—their faces and bodies had always opened into abstract landscapes, just as the abstractions had often embodied the figure in its forms—and in the following months the artist painted a number of abstractions, with highly complex linear interactions. They were exhibited at the Janis Gallery in April 1956 [see Bibliography 7].

It was at this time that wealthy collectors in America and Europe became seriously interested in de Kooning's paintings.

In the winter of 1956–57, the colors and brush strokes in the abstractions grew larger and simpler. By the spring of 1958, a number of canvases, based on small paintings on paper, were finished, in big forms, in thin, clear hues. The series developed through the year, gaining in freshness and scope. They were exhibited at the Janis Gallery in May 1959.

Looking at one of them—a spurt of blue and golden ocher space—de Kooning said recently, "You know, I think I might want to do some Women now."

SELECTED CHRONOLOGICAL BIBLIOGRAPHY
WITH A FEW NOTES

All exhibitions are numbered. Numbers in brackets in front of references to articles and reviews indicate which exhibition is in question.

Statements by the artist and interviews

1937   *Painting and Sculpture in the World of Tomorrow,* a mimeographed prospectus of murals and sculptures for the N.Y. World's Fair prepared by the Fair's publicity department. De Kooning's mural, for the Hall of Pharmacy, is described in terms of its allegory by Michael Loew, who executed another mural for the Hall. (See Chronology).

1949   Letter to the Editor, *Art News,* Jan. 1949; a tribute to Arshile Gorky.

1950   Interview by Martha Bourdrez, *The Knickerbocker,* May 1950; with reflections on Holland and Mondrian.

1951   "The Renaissance and Order," a talk written by de Kooning and delivered as one of a series of lectures by modern artists at Studio 35, New York, in 1950; this important statement was published in *trans/formation,* Vol. 1, #2, 1951.

1951   "What Abstract Art Means to Me," a statement read at a symposium at the Museum of Modern Art, Feb. 5, 1951. It was published by the Museum, along with other artists' statements, in its *Bulletin,* Vol. 18, #3.

1951   Symposium on various topics held in Studio 35, April, 1950; the artist's remarks were recorded and a considerably edited version appeared in *Modern Artists in America* (Wittenborn, Schultz, 1951).

1955   Interview by Storm de Hirsh, largely background color, in *Intro Bulletin,* Oct. 1955.

1958   Interview by T.B.H., "Is today's artist with or against the past," an enquête by *Art News,* June 1958.

One-man exhibitions

1948   **1**   Egan Gallery, N.Y., April 12–May 12 (largely black-and-white paintings, 1946–48).

1951   **2**   Egan Gallery, N.Y., April (1948–51 abstract pictures, many in color).

1951   **3**   Chicago Arts Club, Oct.–Nov. (based on exhibition **2**).

1953   **4**   Janis Gallery, N.Y., March 16–April 11 (*Women*).

1953	5	Boston Museum School, April 21–May 8, retrospective of 20 paintings, 1935–53. The exhibition later traveled to the Workshop Art Center, Washington, D.C., June 13–July 3.
1955	6	Martha Jackson Gallery, N.Y. (catalogue foreword by K. Sawyer), Nov. 9–Dec. 3 (1953–55 pictures, *Women,* a new abstraction).
1956	7	Janis Gallery, April 2–28 (new large abstractions).
1959	8	Janis Gallery, May (new large abstractions).

Joint exhibitions (including several works by de Kooning)

1942	9	McMillen Gallery, N.Y., Jan., with French artists, and Graham, Stuart Davis, Burliuk, Jackson Pollock, Vasilieff; de Kooning showed *Standing Man* (plate 23).
1943	10	Bignou Gallery, N.Y., Feb. 8–Mar. 20, with French artists and Janice Biala, showed *Elegy,* (plate 45) *Pink Landscape,* drawing of Elaine de Kooning (plate 24).
1950	11	Venice Biennale (June–Sept.), small one-man show in American Pavilion organized by Alfred H. Barr, Jr., who also wrote the catalogue foreword; included were *Excavation, Mailbox, Painting 1948.*
1951	12	São Paulo Bienal, organized by the Museum of Modern Art.
1953	13	São Paulo Bienal, organized by the Museum of Modern Art.
1954	14	Venice Biennale (June–Sept.), a retrospective with 26 pictures, 1944–53, selected by Andrew C. Ritchie, for the Museum of Modern Art; he also wrote a catalogue foreword.
1955	15	Whitney Museum, N.Y., "The New Decade," June; illus. catalogue.
1958	16	"The New American Painting," organized by Dorothy Miller of the Museum of Modern Art to tour Europe, then shown at the Museum, June, 1959. Illus. catalogue; foreword by Barr. Included were *Woman I, Woman II, Police Gazette, February 1957.*

A selection of groups shows

De Kooning has been included in almost all surveys of modern art since 1950. The ones mentioned here have interest because of their national importance, or geographical variety, or because the institution in question later bought the painting. In connection with the spread of de Kooning's influence, it should be noted that the Museum of Modern Art included a number of his works in its circulating exhibitions programs.

1936	17	Museum of Modern Art, N.Y., "New Horizons in American Art," work done under the Federal Art Project, W.P.A.; exhibited *Abstraction,* color study, 20 x 14″, for a panel in oil on canvas, 14½ x 19½′.
1948	18	Whitney Museum, "Annual Exhibition of American Painting," Nov. 13–Jan. 4, 1949; included *Mailbox.*
1949	19	Kootz Gallery, N.Y., "The Introspectives," Sept. 14–Oct. 3, included *Attic.*
1949	20	Janis Gallery, Oct., "Husband and Wife" exhibition.
1950	21	Whitney Museum annual, Jan.; *Attic* was hung in a "place of honor."
1950	22	Virginia Museum, Richmond, "American Painting, 1950," chosen by James Johnson Sweeney; *Attic.*
1950	23	Janis Gallery, "Confrontations," U.S. and French paintings, an exhibition prepared to travel to France; Oct. 22–Nov. 13.

1950	24	California Palace of the Legion of Honor, San Francisco, American paintings annual, Nov. 25–Jan. 1, 1951.
1950	25	Whitney Museum annual, Dec., included *Woman*, 1949 (plate 87).
1951	26	Exhibition **23** arrived in Paris, at the Galerie Nina Dausset; catalogue by Mathieu, Tapié, etc. De Kooning classified as a Subjective Expressionist.
1951	27	Museum of Modern Art, "Abstract Painting and Sculpture in America," organized, with catalogue-book, by Andrew C. Ritchie, June–July.
1951	28	Chicago Art Institute, "60th Annual" of American painting and sculpture, Oct. *Excavation* won Logan (1st) prize, $2,000, which the Institute put towards the purchase price of the painting.
1952	29	Janis Gallery, N.Y., "American Vanguard for Paris," Jan.
1952	30	Albright Art Gallery, Buffalo, N.Y., "Expressionism in American Painting," Nov.
1952	31	Galerie de France, Paris, installs exhibition **29**.
1952	32	Carnegie Institute, Pittsburgh, "International" Exhibition, Nov.; included *Boudoir*.
1954	33	Chicago Art Institute, "61st Annual," Oct. 21–Dec. 5; *Woman V.*
1955	34	Carnegie Institute, Pittsburgh "International," Nov., *Woman VI.*
1956	35	Venice Biennale, June–Sept., "American Artists Paint the City," chosen for the Chicago Art Institute by Katherine Kuh; included *Gotham News.*
1957	36	Janis Gallery, N.Y., "8 Americans," April.
1957	37	Albright Art Gallery, Buffalo, N.Y., "Knox Collection," May, exhibits *Gotham News* which it had acquired in 1956.
1957	38	Poindexter Gallery, N.Y., "The '30's Painting in New York," illus. catalogue, edited by Patricia Passloff, with foreword by Edwin Denby, early photograph of de Kooning by Burckhardt, letter from Agnes (Gorky) Phillips (see Chronology).
1958	39	Whitney Museum, "Nature in Abstraction," Jan. 14–March 16; illus. catalogue with many artists' statements, but none from de Kooning, who had put no statements in writing for publication since 1951. *February 1957* was exhibited.
1958	40	Brussels World's Fair, International Exhibition of Modern Art, June–Sept. Illus. catalogue.
1959	41	Janis Gallery, N.Y., "8 Americans," Jan.

Selected reviews of exhibitions

Emphasis is on material that has not been indexed; numbers in brackets refer to the exhibition being discussed in the review.

1942	[9]	*Art Digest,* Jan. 15; illus. *Standing Man* ("a strange painter is William [sic] de Kooning who does anatomical men with one visible eye, but whose work reveals a rather interesting feeling for paint surfaces and color").
1948	[1]	*Art News,* April; illus., by Renée Arb ("His subject [is] the crucial intensity of the creative process itself").
1948	[1]	*PM,* April; illus., by Ad Reinhardt ("not only shows the actual process of creation, but asks the onlooker to 'complete' and 'finish' the painting in the looking act").

1948	[1]	*The Nation*, April 22; by Clement Greenberg ("one of the four or five most important painters in the country . . . magnificent first show").
1948	[1]	*New York Times*, April 25; by Sam Hunter ("interminable fluidity either adds up to an impression of imprisonment with possible contemporary spiritual implications, or one of lugubrious vacillation and paucity of motifs and content, according to your point of view").
1948	[1]	*New York World-Telegram*, May 4; by Emily Genauer ("De Kooning a Puzzle").
1948	[18]	*Art News*, Dec.; by T.B.H. (ambiguity detracts).
1950	[21]	*Art News*, Jan.; illus., by T.B.H. (strength of ambiguity).
1950	[11]	*Art News*, June; illus., by Alfred H. Barr, Jr. foreward to the catalogue of the Venice Biennale, American section (Gorky, de Kooning and Pollock).
1950	[23]	*The Nation*, Nov. 11; by Manny Farber ("a passionate blond nude established on canvas like a Cimabue altarpiece—has the warm density and abandon of a great painting, but draws to a too quick glib completion").
1951	[2]	*Art News*, April; illus., by T.B.H.
1951	[2]	*Art Digest*, April 15.
1951	[2]	*Time*, April 30; illus. (with interview quotations).
1951	[28]	Most of the Chicago daily newspapers, Oct. 23–24, carry stories attacking the "ridiculous" nature of the Chicago Art Institute exhibition and the prize-winning de Kooning picture.
1953	[4]	*Art News*, April; illus., by Henry McBride.
1953	[4]	*Art Digest*, April 1; by Sidney Geist ("monuments of confusion").
1953	[4]	*Art Digest*, April 15; by Hubert Crehan (the critic re-evaluates the *Women*—testimony to the shock these paintings carried when they were first shown).
1953	[4]	*New York Times*, March 22; by Howard Devree.
1953	[4]	*Time*, April ("Big city dames").
1953	[4]	*Arts & Architecture*, May; by James Fitzsimmons (an attack on the notion of ambiguity in de Kooning's painting).
1955	[6]	*Arts*, Nov., illus.; by Leo Steinberg.
1955	[6]	*Art News*, Nov., color illus.; by Fairfield Porter.
1955	[34]	*Life*, Nov. 21, color illus.; *Women VI*, full-page detail.
1955	[6]	*Arts & Architecture*, Dec., illus.; by Dore Ashton.
1956	[7]	*Art News*, April; illus., by T.B.H.
1956	[7]	*Arts*, May.
1956	[7]	*Arts & Architecture*, June; illus., by Dore Ashton.
1956	[35]	*Art News*, Sept.; color illus.
1957	[36]	*Arts & Architecture*, June; by Dore Ashton.
1957	[38]	*Art News*, June; illus., by Clement Greenberg.

Articles and illustrations in periodicals

Most are of a general nature, none of them specifically reviews of exhibitions by de Kooning.

| 1948 | *Magazine of Art*, Feb.; 2 illus., brief biog. |
| 1948 | *Partisan Review*, April; 4 illus., no text. |

1948	*Life,* Oct. 11; Clement Greenberg adduces *Painting 1948* to the round-table discussion on modern art.
1949	*Tiger's Eye,* March; illus. *Orestes,* titled by the editors to fit in a special number on myth.
1950	*Museum of Modern Art Bulletin,* vol. XVII, #2-3; acquisition of *Painting 1948.*
1950	*Magazine of Art,* Oct.; illus., "Marin and de Kooning," by Louis Finkle-stein.
1950	*Art News Annual;* illus. *Introduction to Abstract* by T.B.H.
1951	*Art News,* Jan.; "The New American Action Painting," by Harold Rosenberg.
1953	*Art News,* March; color illus., *Women I,* "De Kooning paints a picture," by T.B.H. (metamorphosis of *Women I*).
1954	*Time,* June 28; color illus., *Woman I.*
1955	*Art News,* April; "Subject: What, How or Who," by Elaine de Kooning (general esthetic discussion).
1955	New York daily newspapers, May 16; "The Public Be Damned," by Huntington Hartford, a full-page advertisement, also carried in many other newspapers throughout the country, which attacked de Kooning with quotes from the *Art News,* March 1953, article. This essay originally appeared in *American Mercury.* In publicity terms, de Kooning was equated with Tennessee Williams and G. C. Menotti.
1955	*Partisan Review,* Spring; " 'American Type' Painting" by Clement Greenberg.
1955	*Art News Annual;* "U.S. Painting: Some Recent Directions," by T.B.H.
1956	*Time,* Feb. 20; color illus., "The Wild Ones," essay on modern U.S. art.
1956	*Baltimore Museum News,* Dec.; illus., "Backyard on Tenth Street," by Kenneth Sawyer.
1958	*Time,* Aug. 4; color illus., essay on American abstract art touring Europe (exhibition 16).
1958	*Horizon,* Sept.; color illus.
1958	*Art News Annual;* color illus., "Tenth Street," by Harold Rosenberg.
1958	*It is,* Summer; color illus.

Books

De Kooning is discussed, or his pictures are illustrated.

1937	John Graham: *System and Dialectics of Art* (Delphic Studios, N.Y., Feb.): "All art produced in America bears the strong unmistakeable stamp of precision or speed . . . Young outstanding American painters: Matulka, Avery, Stuart Davis, Max Weber, David Smith, W. Kooning [sic], Edgar Levy, Boardman Robinson, S. Shane and a few others. Some are just as good and some are better than the leading artists of the same generation in Europe."
1944	Sidney Janis: *Abstract and Surrealist Art in America* (Reynal & Hitchcock, N.Y.), illus. (plate 54).
1946	*Modern Art in Advertising* (Theobold, Chicago), reproduces in color full-page advertisement for *Fortune* which de Kooning executed on commission for the Container Corp., a "watercolor" (probably oil on paper) dated Jan., 1945, of a scene in Holland.
1948	Anton Refregier: *Natural Figure Drawing* (Tudor, N.Y.), illus. (plate 24).

1948	Edwin Denby: *In Public in Private,* poems (Decker, Prairie City, Ill.), frontispiece by de Kooning.
1951	T.B.H.: *Abstract Painting, Background and American Phase* (Viking, N.Y.), 4 illus., 2 in color.
1954	Alfred H. Barr, Jr.: *Masters of Modern Art* (Museum of Modern Art, N.Y.), color illus., *Woman I.*
1955	*Current Biography Yearbook* (Wilson, N.Y.).
1956	Selden Rodman: *The Eye of Man* (Devin-Adair, N.Y.).
1956	Rudi Blesh: *Modern Art U.S.A.* (Knopf N.Y.).
1957	Selden Rodman: *Conversations with Artists* (Delvin-Adair, N.Y.), description of de Kooning's studio. See *Art News,* April 1957, in a review of this book by Herman Cherry, for a contrasting description.
1958	Soby, Miller, Baur, Goodrich: *New Art in America* (N.Y. Graphic & Praeger), color illus., *Woman I,* comments by Soby.
1958	Alexander Eliot: *American Painting* (Time, Inc.), color illus., *Woman I.*
1958	Sam Hunter and others: *Art since 1945* (Abrams, N.Y.), color illus., *Woman I.*
1958	*Painters and poets, a portfolio* (Weisenthal & Grippe, Morris Gallery, N.Y.), de Kooning etching for the poem *Revenge* by Harold Rosenberg.
1959	Dust jacket for the book *Tradition of the New* by Harold Rosenberg (Horizon, N.Y.).

Postscript to the chronological bibliography

De Kooning has always been a generous lender to group exhibitions, especially those organized by artists themselves—many of which have been too ephemeral to record. He contributed from its beginning in 1951 to the "Artists' Co-operative Annual," which opened in an empty Ninth Street store in 1951, and later moved for a few seasons to the Stable Gallery. He also lent pictures to the Tanager Gallery, St. Mark's Church and innumerable other organizations.

Practically every serious exhibition of American art since 1950 has included at least one de Kooning (e.g. Walker Art Center, Minneapolis; Guggenheim Museum, New York); lack of space prevents a complete listing.

European dealers by around 1952 had a few de Koonings which they added to group exhibitions in Paris, Rome, Zurich, Milan, etc.

The International program of the Museum of Modern Art has circulated de Koonings to Asia and throughout Europe, in addition to the exhibition (16) already mentioned.

Prof. William Seitz of Princeton University has an unpublished Ph.D. thesis on Abstract-Expressionism in America, and documentation on the artist.

Prof. Meyer Schapiro of Columbia University has assigned a number of graduate students over the years to do papers on de Kooning.

I am informed that Harriet Janis and Rudi Blesh are engaged in a book on de Kooning (Grove Press, N.Y.).

Poems on paintings by de Kooning have been written by Frank O'Hara, Harold Rosenberg, Jascha Kessler, Ida Fox.

A documentary film (11 minutes) on de Kooning was made in April 1956 by Sidney Hantman, Marvin Goldman and Irving Sandler.

Scrap-books at the Janis Gallery, N.Y., comprise a fairly comprehensive file of press notices since 1953. I have had to omit many recent press notices for reasons of space.

INDEX OF PLATES

The roman numerals refer to text references, the *italic* numerals to the black and white plates, and the **bold face** numerals to the color plates. The titles of the reproductions are listed in *italics*. The first reference is the plate number.

125

INDEX OF NAMES AND SUBJECTS